52 CALIFORNIA ROCKIN' ROAD TRIPS

AN ECO-TOUR GUIDE AND TRAVEL JOURNAL

YouTopo

52 CALIFORNIA ROCKIN' ROAD TRIPS: AN ECO-TOUR GUIDE AND TRAVEL JOURNAL
WRITTEN BY: DAVID POWELL
WRITING CONTRIBUTORS: CAROLINE POWELL, LOREN TUCKER, ELIZA POWELL
EDITED BY: CAROLINE POWELL, CAROLYN POWELL, ELIZA POWELL
PHOTOGRAPHS BY: SEE PHOTOGRAPHY CREDITS PAGE 227-228
DESIGN BY: DAVID POWELL, PABLO AIRTH, DEREK TAMAYO
ILLUSTRATIONS BY: JAMAYAL TANWEER, MILBETH MORILLO, DEREK TAMAYO, PABLO AIRTH
ART DIRECTION: DAVID POWELL AND PABLO AIRTH
COVER DESIGN: PABLO AIRTH

FIRST EDITION

VISIT: ***WWW.YOUTOPO.COM***

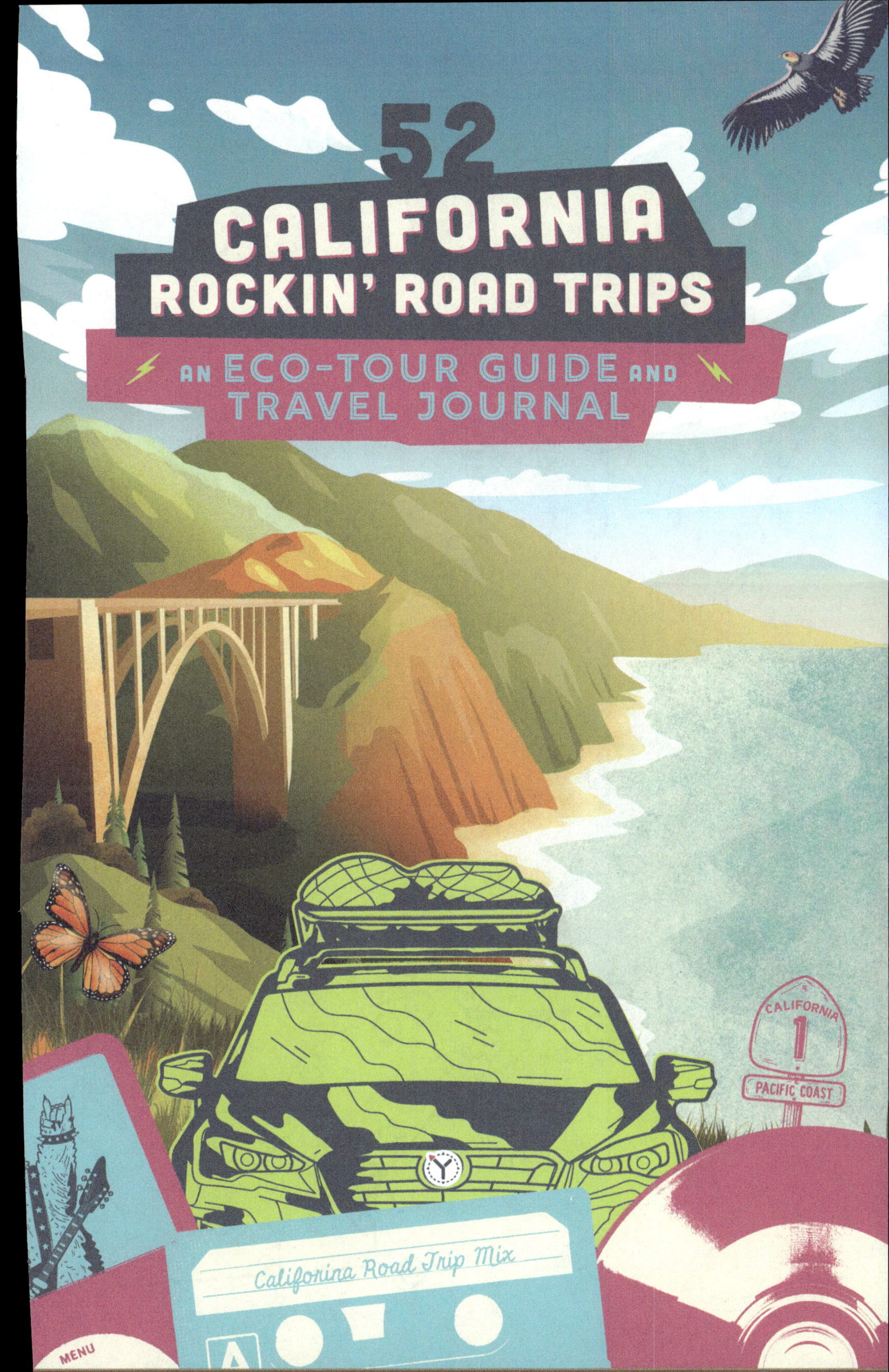
52
CALIFORNIA
ROCKIN' ROAD TRIPS
AN ECO-TOUR GUIDE AND
TRAVEL JOURNAL
CALIFORNIA
1
PACIFIC COAST
Califorina Road Trip Mix
MENU

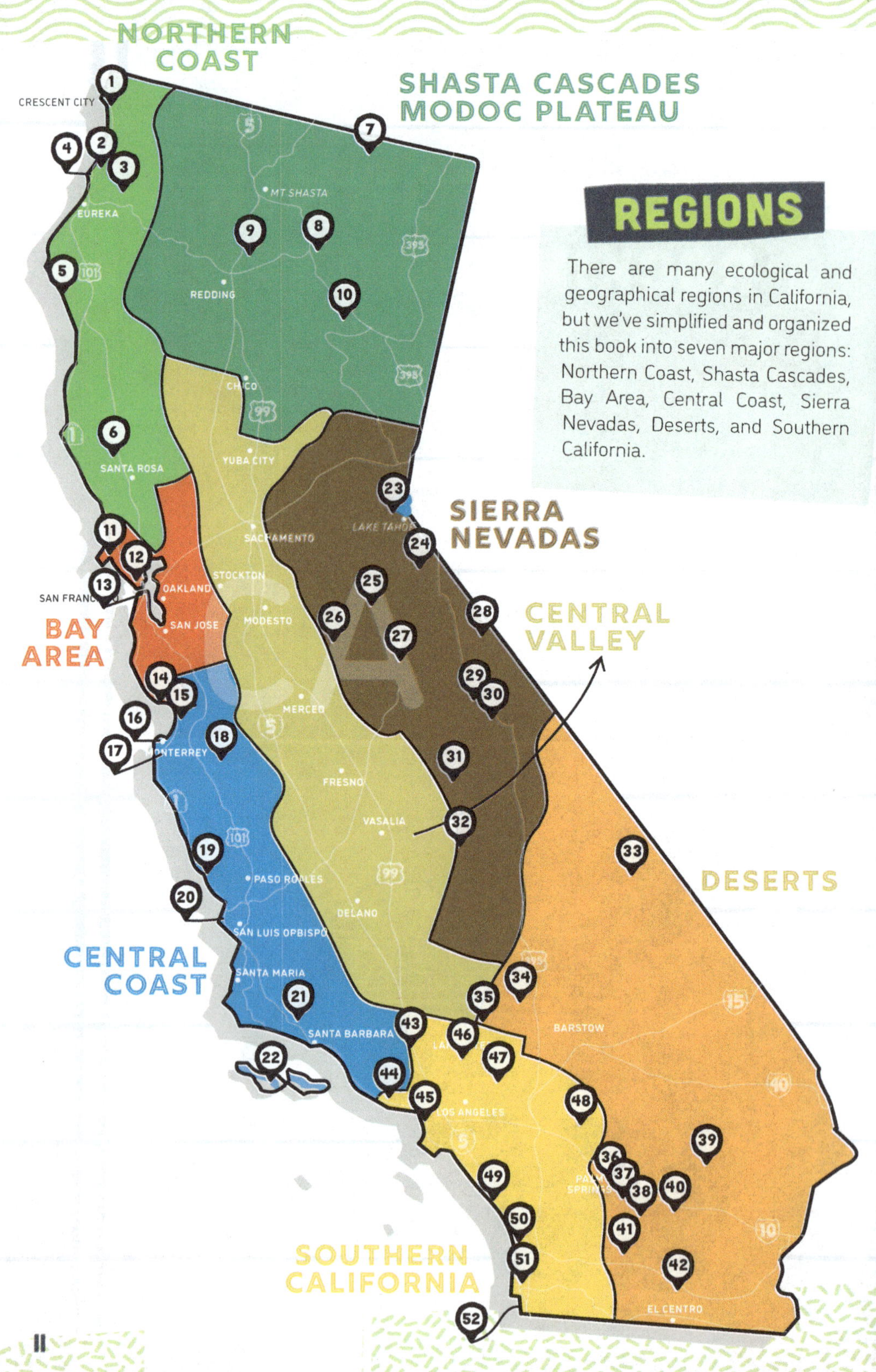
NORTHERN COAST
SHASTA CASCADES MODOC PLATEAU
REGIONS
There are many ecological and geographical regions in California, but we've simplified and organized this book into seven major regions: Northern Coast, Shasta Cascades, Bay Area, Central Coast, Sierra Nevadas, Deserts, and Southern California.
SIERRA NEVADAS
CENTRAL VALLEY
BAY AREA
DESERTS
CENTRAL COAST
SOUTHERN CALIFORNIA
CRESCENT CITY
EUREKA
MT SHASTA
REDDING
CHICO
YUBA CITY
SANTA ROSA
SACRAMENTO
LAKE TAHOE
STOCKTON
OAKLAND
SAN FRANCISCO
SAN JOSE
MODESTO
MERCED
MONTERREY
FRESNO
VASALIA
PASO ROBLES
DELANO
SAN LUIS OPBISPO
SANTA MARIA
SANTA BARBARA
BARSTOW
LOS ANGELES
PALM SPRINGS
EL CENTRO
CA

TABLE OF CONTENTS

View
MENU

INTRODUCTION

CALIFORNIA IS A BIG PLACE! 163,696 square miles with 840 miles of coastline. It's also the most geologically diverse state in the United States with towering mountains, volcanic activity, beautiful beaches, islands, forests, deserts, caves, cliffs, rivers, wetlands, marshes, tidepools, estuaries, active fault lines, and an abundance of diverse living creatures."There are approximately 30,000 species of insects, 63 of freshwater fish, 46 amphibians, 96 reptiles, 563 birds, 190 mammals, and more than 8,000 plants". It's an outdoor wonderland for adventure seekers and nature lovers. Climbing, hiking, surfing, skiing, fishing, birding....whatever you're looking for, you can pretty much find it in California.

The creation and design of this book is inspired by the great diversity of California. We wanted to create a fun, engaging, creative book that would inspire and connect people to the best places and to learn about the wildlife that call those places home. The idea was to fill the book with fun written and visual content. This book project contains everything we love: family, adventure, nature, and music. The project also includes a video series for every destination to get you excited and inspired to have these adventures yourself. The book also includes original hand drawings, artwork, scavenger hunts, bits of history, spots to record notes, and links to additional online resources. You can also find the posters of the artwork and coloring books of this California collection at youtopo.com.

On a personal note, this project was born during the "covid years." Our family of 5 has spent the past few years traveling in the tight quarters of an RV using the entire state of California as our big backyard. As a California native and having lived all over the state throughout my life, there is a real attachment and genuine love for this special place. My fondest memories growing up were family vacations and scouting trips spent camping at places like Yosemite, searching for crickets in meadows, climbing on rocks, surfing it's ocean shores, snowboarding it's mountain slopes, and enjoying its year round amazing weather. As a professional Landscape Architect I also have a passion for our environment and learning about how we can protect it. It's been a labor of love to visit all of these places with my family and to create this project.

The main goal of this book is to help people get stoked about engaging and learning about nature through fun adventures. When there is stoke, there is love. And when we love things, we take care of them. The planet needs more people who truly love and care for it. The planet needs a generation of humans that are passionate about finding solutions to help protect our environment. Our philosophy is that the best way for that to happen is to get more people outside and connected to nature in fun, curious, and engaging ways that cultivate a great love for our earth. So get out there and let the stoke begin!

ROCK ON!
David Powell,
YouTopo

WHAT'S INSIDE

PRO TIPS: These include things like best season to visit, difficulty of activity, cost of trip, time needed, and other details to help plan your trip and have a great adventure.

TOP 5 HITS: These are activities we recommend for families. It typically does not include the highly technical and difficult hikes that young adventurers would not be able to manage. But go where your curiosity, interests, and ability take you and don't be a slave to a bucketlist... enjoying the journey is more meaningful than being overly focused on the destination.

PLAYLIST: Use the QR codes found for each location playlist. You can watch a fun video for each destination, find music playlists, link to other online resources, see maps, and shop for fun goodies to make your trip even more memorable.

LINER NOTES: This is where you'll get a bit of background and history about this place. Learning about each place will enrich your adventure and help you feel a greater connection to each destination.

MEET THE LOCALS: This section is for learning about what you might see on your adventure. It includes plants, animals, rocks, and formations that call this place home. It can also be treated as a Scavenger Hunt to keep both adults and kids engaged. Lots of kids don't appreciate going for a "hike"... but just having them be on the lookout for specific plants or animals is one way to get them more interested and engaged. When you are curious about plants you see, take a picture or make a sketch. You can use online resources like inaturalist.org or cnps.org to identify which plant you've found.

SHOW NOTES: This is a spot to take a few brief notes or doodle about what made your trip fun. Your future self will appreciate it. Maybe you had a close encounter with wildlife or felt a great sense of love or wonder for nature. Writing it down will help ensure that this special memory is etched in your brain as well as on paper.

REWARDS: Yes, just being in the beautiful outdoors is a reward in and of itself... but remember to reward young kids (and adults) when completing a hike or adventure. It could be a special treat you love or "earning" some screen time. Use positive reinforcement to associate being active in nature as a good thing!

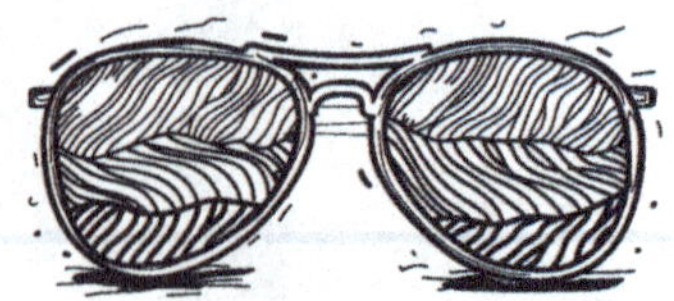

ECO-LICIOUS

GET FAMILIAR WITH YOUR SURROUNDINGS: The whole "eco" part of this book refers to ecology. Ecology is the study of how organisms relate to one another and their surroundings. That includes everything from microorganisms to plants and animals. In the natural world everything is connected and co-dependant. As humans we like to believe that nature is something separate and "out there." But as much as we try to distance ourselves and detach ourselves from nature, we will always be connected to this place called earth. Its future is our future. If something is bad for the earth it's bad for humans. There is no getting around that. This book is intended to 1) get you out in nature, 2) learn a bit about where you're going and what lives there, and 3) have fun doing it. Be sure to be respectful during your adventures by minimizing your impact. You can do this by staying on designated trails, keeping a safe distance from animals, packing out all of your trash, and picking up other litter you find.

MINIMIZE YOUR IMPACT DURING TRAVEL: Everything we do has some impact on the environment, including travel. To help offset our impact of travel try using more environmentally sustainable products in your travels like; reusable metal straws (500 million straws are thrown in the trash every single day....in the U.S. alone), reusable water bottles (480 billion single use plastic water bottles thrown away every year in the world) , utensils, or shopping bags. You could camp instead of staying in a hotel. Reducing consumption of high impact foods (livestock is responsible for 18 percent of all human-caused greenhouse gas emissions) is another way to reduce our environmental impact when you eat out. Check out habitsofwaste.com for more info on the impact of our consumption on the planet and how we can all make a difference through small changes to our habits.

CALIFORNIA ECOSYSTEMS: California is an incredibly diverse landscape, so understanding the various ecosystems (the study of how organisms relate to one another and their surroundings) is no small task. The systems in nature that can be found in California include: shallow rock reefs and kelp forests, intertidal, estuaries, sandy beaches, coastal dunes, coastal sage scrub, grasslands, chaparral, oak woodlands, coast redwood forests, montane forests, subalpine forests, alpine, deserts, wetlands, lakes, and rivers. And there are also sub-groups found within those categories. The goal of this book is not to become an expert biologist on defining ecosystems, but rather to experience them, have adventures, and learn a bit about each area you visit. If you're wanting to dig deeper into these ecosystems, the best book on this vast subject is Ecosystems of California by Harold Mooney and Erika Zavaleta (Editors). It's a comprehensive and thorough read intended for college level studies, so if you're interested in a more accessible introductory book we highly recommend The California Naturalist Handbook by Adina Merenlender, Deborah Stanger Edelman, and Greg de Nevers.

SCAN FOR BOOK RECOMMENDATIONS

PLANT COMMUNITIES: Plant communities are part of ecosystems and are groups of plants typically found together in similar environments. All ecosystems listed in the previous subsection have associated plant communities but we'll focus on the more general categories associated with plant communities. Great online resources include the California Native Plant Society (cnps.org) where you can learn more about native plants through their online database, books, publications, and workshops. It's a tremendous resource for those interested in learning about California's native plants, how to protect them, and how to plant them in your own gardens. Another good resource for learning about native plant communities is wildlife.ca.gov where you can find online map databases available to the government and the public. We've highlighted hundreds of plants for you to find on your adventures so you can learn about the beautiful and diverse life that you're experiencing. Take a few minutes and read about them before you head out on your adventure. QR code to page links

FORESTS: Forested lands cover a third of California (cnps.org) and include a mix of various forest types such as redwood forest, mixed-evergreen forest, coniferous forest, riparian forest, closed-cone pine forest, douglas-fir forest, and montane forests. These plant communities have a nearly continuous canopy and are found at higher elevations of the state or in Northern California.

COASTAL SAGE SCRUB: Also called "soft chaparral" since it's leaves are typically softer than the hard, waxy leaves of similar chaparral. This low-growing plant community is typically adapted to the coastal lowlands and varies as you move from northern to southern coastal regions of the state. Species include: California sagebrush, golden yarrow, white sage, California buckwheat, lemonade berry, and toyon.

DESERTS: The two main desert plant communities include Desert Scrub (examples include: Great Basin sagebrush, desert beargrass, mojave yucca) and Desert Woodland (species include: desert willow, palo verde, desert lavender).

MONTANE MEADOWS: These are typically temporary landscapes that exist at higher elevations (4,000' plus) in ranges such as the Sierra-Cascade ranges in areas of moisture where water may have been or is receding such as ponds and lakes. They appear after snowmelt and disappear when dry. They're a magical mix of wildflowers, sedges, and perennial bunchgrasses and can be filled with pollinators. The palette varies greatly throughout the state but can include species such as lupines, corn lily, red-heather, and meadow paintbrush.

ALPINE:

Above the tree line in high elevation mountain ranges of the Sierra Nevadas, the plants found here are 90% perennials and are characterized by small, low-growing, mat morning plants. You can find flowers blooming in these harsh weather and rock environments such as dwarf mountain fleabane, Anderson mountain crown, and spreading phlox.

WOODLAND / OAK SAVANNA:

The woodland plant community found throughout California is found at lower elevations and interior valleys of the Coast, Transverse, and Peninsular Ranges, with the majestic oak as star of the show (dominance varies between regions) with significant gaps in tree canopies. The more dominant oaks include the coast live oak, valley oak, white oak, black oak (you think they would have gotten more creative with the naming of these beauties.) Other vegetation include shrubs such as coffeeberry, hummingbird sage and large expanses of grasses (mostly invasive exotic annuals). Sadly most Oak Woodlands in California are seriously threatened by human development.

GRASSLANDS:

Grasslands cover a large portion of California extending from coast regions, across the great Central Valley, and up to the edges of the Sierras. Sadly, nearly all of California's native perennial bunchgrasses have been overtaken by invasive annual grasses (brought from overseas or embedded in livestock) or destroyed by human development. Unlike the exotic annual grasses that dry up with the seasonal rain, California native perennial bunchgrasses like deer grass, needlegrass, and blue-eyed grass held color and textures that would continue year round. Still, grasslands can explode with color as wildflowers display their seasonal bloom in species such as California poppy, goldfields, tidy-tips and lupine.

CHAPARRAL:

Typically characterized by shrub-dominated plants with thick, small, evergreen leaves. They live in coastal foothills and mountain slopes between 500 and 4500 elevation that are hot and dry. Their design, form, and even chemical composition reflect how they've adapted to fire and drought conditions. Some of the species include sugar bush, toyon, manzanita, ceanothus and are mostly identified in Mediterranean climate zones.

RIPARIAN ZONES: These are places where water naturally flows either year round or seasonally. It could be a bank of a river, stream, or lake. It's a reliable source of water for plants so you'll often see an abundance of life, both tall and small. A canopy of trees such as cottonwoods, alders, sycamores, or smaller trees/ shrubs such as willows, dogwoods, and birches. In the understory you might find rushes, wild morning glory, and honeysuckle. These species will vary greatly depending on where you go.

WETLANDS: In general, these are places connected to streams, rivers, lakes, and oceans. They can occur across all types of biomes. Some of the different types of wetlands include bogs, vernal pools, baylands, marshes, sloughs, swamps, fens, and estuaries. Studies show that anywhere from 75%-90% of California's original wetlands have been lost. How tragic! These important natural "sponges" help provide habitat, improve water quality, provide erosion control, and increase water supply. They're also great places to go bird watching and find cool plants like the cobra plant, lady ferns, cattails, and giant tules.

CALIFORNIA SEASONS: All year Baby! California is amazing because there are destinations available year round no matter what your temperature and weather preference is. Typically California is known for having cool wet winters and long, dry summers. But it's such a big and diverse landscape that it all depends on when and where you are.

WINTER: The winter is special throughout much of the state because the dry, golden hills come to life with winter rains. It can bring annual wildflower blooms and colorful flowers to natives such as hummingbird sage, gooseberry, manzanita, and chaparral currant. California isn't as well-known for seasonal color like New England but you will find bright fall yellows from big-leaf maples in the north, aspens in the mountains, and red berries of toyon in the south. Winter is a great time to visit the desert and southern areas if you're looking to escape the cold. You can also hit the slopes in the Sierras and San Bernardino Mountains if you want to escape the heat. California is famous for being able to ski and surf on the same day!

SPRING: Like most places, spring is a great season for wildflower blooms, waterfalls, and seasonal rivers. Get a front row seat to Yosemite Falls or float down the Smith River in Jedediah Smith Redwoods State Park. Hike the trails and you can find bright orange blooms of bush monkeyflower, johnny jump-ups, baby blue-eyes and of course the famous California poppies which can blanket hillsides when followed by a wet winter. Take a hike along the coast and you might see red larkspur, western dog violets, Indian paintbrush, and buckwheat.

SUMMER: Summer is the dry season and much plant life goes dormant, but it's a great time for higher-elevation adventures. Most of California will get little to no rainfall from June until October. Hillsides turn golden and fire season comes into play. Fire is a natural and important part of the California landscape. Many California native plants actually need fire to thrive. Sequoias trees rely on fire to release most seeds from their cones. But due to a century of management built strictly to suppress fire, we see overloaded fuel levels that can break out in dangerous and deadly "mega fires." If you're on the coast you'll likely experience "June Gloom" as morning fog fills the air and soon burns off. During this season you might find white blooms of western azalea, ninebark, and matilija poppy...or blues and purple from woolly blue curls and cleveland sage. Of course there's no better season to relax on a warm sandy beach than a nice summer day.

FALL: Fall is a great time to go anywhere in the Golden State. Head to the desert or the mountains with overall comfortable weather. California is still clinging to summer weather in September. Some early migrating birds forage, deer browse where they can, and pink clarkias and pacific asters shine in coastal gardens. The Santa Ana winds in the south begin to blow as cool, high-pressure desert air collides with the low-pressure coastal air.

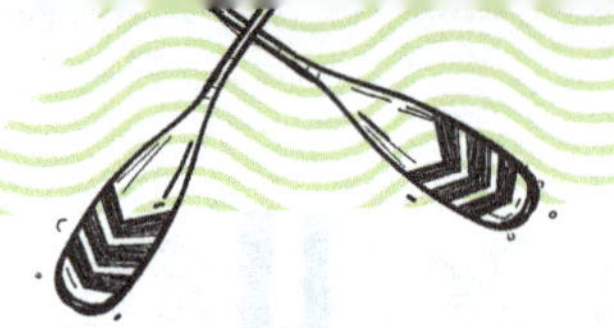

SAFETY FIRST

LIVE ANOTHER DAY: Don't be that person taking risky photos just for an Instagram picture. Have adventures that challenge you but are within your skill level. Or just take a relaxing stroll in nature to enjoy the sights and sounds. It doesn't always have to be about pushing your limits; it can just be for pure enjoyment and relaxation.

HYDRATE: Avoid long hikes on hot days with lots of full-sun exposure. Don't make the mistake of not packing enough water for everyone.

POWER SNACKS: Always keep plenty of snacks on hand. "Hangry" (hungry and angry) people are not fun people. You're burning lots of calories when you're out there hiking, so make sure you're keeping fuel in the tank.

FLASH LIGHTS: Night hikes or star gazing is definitely recommended, but be prepared and pack a flashlight. It never hurts to be prepared even if you think you don't need it.

SUNSCREEN AND INSECT REPELLENT: Be prepared with sunblock and insect repellent to make sure your experience isn't tainted by sun burns and bites. Just remember that if you have any chemicals on your hands not to touch or engage with any amphibians as it will harm them since their skin is permeable.

CHECK THE STATUS: Depending on the season and weather, certain adventures might not be open. Go online or call before you go.

TOP 50 CALIFORNIA HITS

Any good road trip needs some good tunage. That is why we used music as a metaphorical concept and visual tool to weave and tie together this project. Why are there so many great songs about California? No other state can put together such an impressive catalog of music. As Neil Young says "I've been to Hollywood, I've been to Redwood." It's a land of gold that we can mine over and over again. Here are our "Top 52" songs about California to groove to while you hit the road. Note to music fans; We've intentionally left off some really good songs to keep it clean and family friendly.

1. *CALIFORNIA SOUL, MARLENA SHAW*
2. *CALIFORNIA STARS, BILLY BRAGG, WILCO*
3. *CALIFORNIA, JONI MITCHELL*
4. *DANI CALIFORNIA, THE RED HOT CHILI PEPPERS*
5. *GOING TO CALIFORNIA, LED ZEPPELIN*
6. *HOTEL CALIFORNIA, THE EAGLES*
7. *CALIFORNIA DREAMIN', THE MAMAS & THE PAPAS*
8. *CALIFORNIA GIRLS, THE BEACH BOYS*
9. *CALIFORNIA SUN, THE RAMONES*
10. *HEART OF GOLD, NEIL YOUNG*
11. *QUEEN OF CALIFORNIA, JOHN MAYER*
12. *BEVERLY HILLS, WEEZER*
13. *SITTIN ON THE DOCK OF THE BAY, OTIS REDDING*
14. *CALIFORNIA, PHANTOM PLANET*
15. *CALIFORNIA, MASON JENNINGS*
16. *SAN FRANCISCO, SCOTT MCKENZIE*
17. *BIG SUR, THE THRILLS*
18. *L.A. WOMAN, THE DOORS*
19. *CALIFORNIA WAITING, KINGS OF LEON*
20. *INTO THE CALIFORNIA SUN, THE RIVIERAS*
21. *SAN FRANCISCO, FOXYGEN*
22. *CALIFORNIA BLUE, ROY ORBISON*
23. *ROUTE 66, CHUCK BERRY*
24. *SURFIN' U.S.A., THE BEACH BOYS*
25. *BACK TO CALIFORNIA, CAROLE KING*
26. *CALIFORNICATION, RED HOT CHILI PEPPERS*
27. *ALL I WANT TO DO, SHERLY CROW*
28. *PACIFIC COAST HIGHWAY, AWOLNATION FEATURING WEEZER*
29. *IT NEVER RAINS IN SOUTHERN CALIFORNIA, ALBERT HAMMOND*
30. *CALIFORNIA (CAST IRON SOUL), JAMESTOWN REVIVAL*
31. *VENTURA HIGHWAY, AMERICA*
32. *MEET ME IN CALIFORNIA, PLAIN WHITE TS*
33. *CALIFORNIA ENGLISH PT 2, VAMPIRE WEEKEND*
34. *I LEFT MY WALLET IN EL SEGUNDO, A TRIBE CALLED QUEST*
35. *FREE FALLIN, TOM PETTY*
36. *PROMISED LAND, CHUCK BERRY*
37. *CALIFORNIA'S CALLIN ME, MIKE O'ROURKE*
38. *CALIFORNIA I'M COMIN, LITTLE RICHARD BAND*
39. *REDWOOD TREE, VAN MORRISON*
40. *GOING BACK TO CALI, LL COOL J*
41. *HIGHWAY 101, SOCIAL DISTORTION*
42. *CALIFORNIA (ALL THE WAY), LUNA*
43. *TO CALIFORNIA, THE MIGHTY MIGHTY BOSSTONES*
44. *PRETTY GIRL FROM SAN DIEGO, THE AVETT BROTHERS*
45. *SAN FRANCISCO, THE MOWGLI'S*
46. *CALIFORNIA SKY, UNWRITTEN LAW*
47. *SANTA CRUZ, PEARL JAM*
48. *COMING INTO LOS ANGELES, ARLO GUTHRIE*
49. *BACK IN CALIFORNIA, MIKE PINTO*
50. *I LOVE L.A., RANDY NEWMAN*

SCAN FOR CALIFORNIA PLAYLIST

CHECK OUT OUR SITE

YouTopo.com

ROCK STAR MERCH:

Find your favorite National Park Tour shirt in many sizes and colors.

COLORING AND ACTIVITYBOOKS:

Geek out on nature with our coloring and activity books!
YouTopo.com + Amazon.com

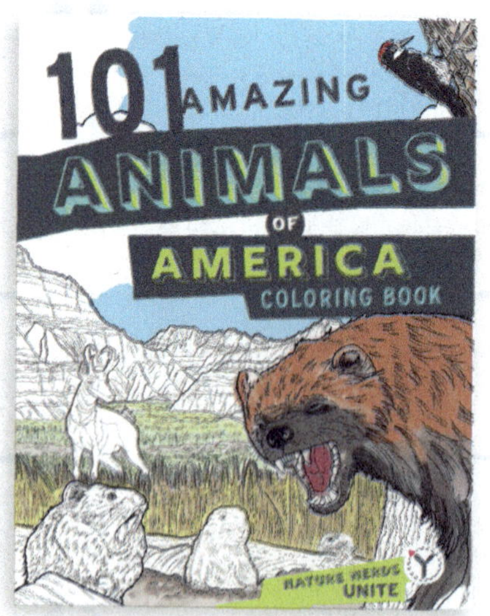

Find your favorite California Dreamin' poster at **YouTopo.com**

CALIFORNIA DREAMIN' POSTERS:

NATIONAL PARK TOUR: ROCK STAR POSTERS

Check out the full National Park Tour catalogue at **YouTopo.com**

NORTHERN COAST

The biggest star of the Northern Coast would have to be the Redwoods that blanket the landscape and shade its rivers. Redwoods have been here for an estimated 20 million years and are the tallest living species on earth. A great place to see these giants is Redwood National Park (who would have thought?). In this region you can also visit the majestic Fern Canyon, where salamanders, frogs, and banana slugs (the second largest slug in the world) stay moist and cool in a narrow canyon with walls completely covered by ferns and moss. Stroll beautiful black sand beaches at Shelter Cove in a strip of coastline known as the "The Lost Coast." Take a ride down the Smith River, the only major, free-flowing river in California where salmon go to lay their eggs. Or just take a lazy float down the Russian River. If you want to see some of the best tidepools in the state then Sue-Meg State Park is a must see for gumboot chiton and huge sea anemones. The Northern Coast is a fantastic place to take a rockin' road trip for the whole family. You won't be disappointed.

TOP 5 HITS

1. Hike the Stout Grove trail, .5 mile.
2. Kayak the Smith River.
3. Hike the Simpson-Reed Grove Trail, .9 mile.
4. Visit the estuary where the river meets the ocean to see sea lions and birds. GPS 41.948037, -124.205010 cross streets- Mouth of Smith River Road and Rivers End Road.
5. Attend a park Interpretive Activity (summer only)

PRO TIPS

Season: Fun all year round; salmon spawning happens fall after the first big rains

Difficulty: Easy. The water is calm for kayaking near Jedediah State Park, and the rapids are mild (Class I). Call Redwood Rides for kayaking in this area--they are the only company that does kayaking in this area of the river. Talk to them about what would be appropriate for your family skill level. Yes, beginners are okay.

Time Needed: Full day

- Call Redwood Rides for kayaking in this area--they are the only company that is licensed to offer kayaking in this area of the river. Talk to them about what would be appropriate for your family skill level. Class 1-2 rapids Yes, beginners are okay.
- If kayaking you will get wet; have fun and enjoy it.
- You can rent kayaks from Redwood Rides or do a guided paddle.
- Stop at rocky shore areas in spring and summer to picnic and look for tadpoles.
- You can leave your kayaks on shore and hike around the Stout Grove Trail, but it's better to drive to the Stout Grove after kayaking so you can take your time exploring and not feel rushed.
- When exploring the Stout Grove take your time and look closely at ferns and fallen trees. Check out sori on the ferns or spot a banana slug feasting on decaying matter.
- A fun place to swim in the river is the Society Hole off HWY 199. Address is 6441 North Bank Road Jedediah Smith Redwoods State Park, Crescent City, CA 95531
- Take binoculars to the estuary on Mouth of Smith River Road. Wildlife can be seen from the beach. There are no bathrooms located here.
- The rock bed located where Mill Creek meets the Smith river is a prime spawning ground for salmon Oct.- Feb. Do not walk on it if the river water is covering the rocks. You can crush young salmon and eggs. Mill Creek is located on the edge of the Stout Grove.

kayak the Smith River

VIDEOS AND RESOURCES

SHOW NOTES

The Smith River is the last large natural free flowing river in California. This means there are no dams along the length of the river. It is cold, clear, and rocky, perfect for salmon spawning. The large growing redwoods and other trees keep the river shaded and cool year round, perfect temperatures for salmon. As the Save the Redwoods League says, with "thick redwood forests, banana slugs, a beautiful river, and pollywogs, what more could you ask for?"

Unlike many other rivers, the Smith River is not fed by snow melt. Instead, areas of the river receive around 100 inches of rain per year. This rain collects into small rivers and streams that then flow into the Smith River. The junction where Mill Creek flows into the Smith River in Jedediah Smith State Park is a prime spawning ground for coho salmon. In the fall and winter, the water rises, covering the rocky shore line and making it a perfect place for the salmon to lay their eggs.

MY PLAYLIST

music, books, podcasts...

SUGGESTED JAM

Track: California (Pt. II)

Artist: Mason Jennings

MEET THE LOCALS

get to know the flora, fauna and features

JEDEDIAH SMITH STATE PARK

COASTAL REDWOOD

The coastal redwood is the tallest tree on earth and can grow around 300 feet. They grow quickly which helps them capture more CO2 from our vehicles and power plants than any other tree on Earth. If a redwood is cut down, it will release stored CO2 back into the air.

TADPOLE

Tadpoles (pollywogs) are baby frogs that can be found along shallow, slower water. These babies are born with gills to breathe underwater and a tail used for swimming and finding algae to eat. Tadpoles are fun to find and catch, but remember to keep them wet and put them back.

REDWOOD SORREL

Redwoods love shade and have edible, clover-shaped leaves (0.4 to two inches long). These leaves have a tangy, lemony flavor but are mildly toxic, so they should only be eaten in small quantities. Native American tribes still use this plant as a garnish for dried fish and as a type of medicine.

SWORD FERN

The sword fern can grow up to four feet tall and lives in cool, shady areas. Its leaves look large and tough compared to other ferns. If you look at the underside of its leaves, you might find orange or yellow spots. These are spores called "sori" that the fern uses to reproduce.

RIVER ROCK FOR SPAWNING

Salmon dig nests in the shallow, cool, rocky river beds, where they lay their eggs. Once the eggs are laid and fertilized, the female salmon buries the eggs with rocks to protect them. Spawning grounds can be found by Stout Grove where Mill Creek meets the Smith River.

MY REVIEW

Write about your experience

2

PRO TIPS

Season: Year round, early morning for parking and less crowds

Difficulty: Easy

Time Needed: Half day

- Join Frog Watch USA to learn how families can help frogs. (https://www.aza.org/frogwatch)
- Visit early morning before 10 a.m. or late afternoon/evening to beat the crowds. The parking lot is small.
- Take your time to explore; look around everywhere for frogs and salamanders. Garter snakes, small fish, and banana slugs can also be found. Look but don't touch.
- Wear water shoes, the walk through Fern Canyon crosses Home Creek several times. Some planks and small bridges are placed in the creek to help you walk.
- Go to the restroom before you leave the parking lot.
- Walk the length of the canyon more than once.
- Visit Trillium Falls. If you have small kids--walk the trail counterclockwise to the falls and double back the way you came. This is about one mile total. The full loop is 3.1 miles.
- Look down at your feet as you hike to see yellow spotted millipedes.

TOP 5 HITS

1. Hike the amazing Fern Canyon, 1.1 mile loop, and look for amphibians (like salamanders and frogs) hiding under leaves and in water.
2. Climb on fallen logs to gain a new perspective.
3. Visit and picnic at Gold Bluffs Beach.
4. Hike to Trillium Falls, 3.1 mile loop.
5. Watch for Roosevelt elk in the Elk Meadow.

Walk the plank mate

SHOW NOTES

A can't-miss site in Prairie Creek Redwoods State Park, Fern Canyon is named for the myriad of ferns that blanket its nearly vertical 50-foot walls. Ferns are unique plants that first began to grow on Earth over 300 million years ago, making them even older than dinosaurs!

The ferns at Fern Canyon belong to more than seven different species, all fed by water trickling down the sides of the canyon. Water is so plentiful here that you might notice the cascades of moss growing down the walls of the narrow gorge dripping with water. The Home Creek, which through time has carved this ravine, flows down the center of the canyon. The presence of all this moisture (and the resulting ferns and mosses that trap it in) creates a damp, rainforest-like microclimate in which amphibians such as frogs and salamanders can thrive.

VIDEOS AND RESOURCES

MY PLAYLIST

music, books, podcasts...

SUGGESTED JAM

Track: Queen of California

Artist: John Mayer

MEET THE LOCALS

get to know the flora, fauna and features

FERN CANYON

FIVE FINGER FERN

The five finger fern can grow up to three feet tall. The leaves that grow on its black stems form a finger like pattern. These ferns were used by the Yurok tribe to make baskets. They believed picking ferns from the same patch each year would stimulate more growth for the following year.

LADY FERNS

Lady ferns can grow between two and five feet tall, producing stems that can be green, purple, or even red in color. These plants are deciduous ferns, meaning they drop their leaves with the first frost of the year. Unlike most other ferns, these can tolerate the sun and survive in dry soil.

NORTHERN RED-LEGGED FROG

Northern red-legged frogs range from rusty brown to gray-green on their backs, with dark spots and reddish coloring on their undersides. The call of a northern red-legged frog makes a "uh-uh-uh-uh-uh" sound. These frogs are insectivores, meaning they only eat insects.

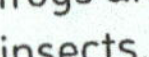

ENSATINA SALAMANDER

The ensatina salamander is a three to five inch long, lungless salamander, meaning it breathes entirely through its skin! If a predator grabs its tail, it will come off, and the ensatina will grow a new one. A milky white substance secreted from its tail also repels predators.

WAVY-LEAVED COTTON MOSS

Wavy-leaved cotton moss tends to look like a shag rug. It has flattened, spear-shaped stems and can appear shiny. The dripping waterfalls of Fern Canyon are perfect for this plant, which loves moist, shaded areas. You can also find it on moist soil, humus, and decaying logs along streams.

MY REVIEW

Write about your experience

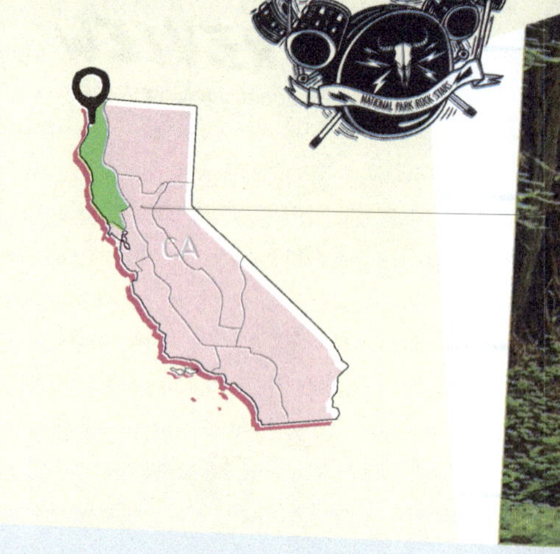

PRO TIPS

Season: Spring or summer (to see elk calves)

Time Needed: 1-2 days

Difficulty: Easy

Time Needed: 1-2 days

- Take your time on the Revelation Sensory Trail. It's a great place to touch, smell, listen, see, and even taste the forest.
- Another great place to see Roosevelt elk is in the fields next to Elk Country Campground.
- Picnic or take a drive along Newton B Drury Scenic Parkway to take a break from hiking.
- The tallest tree in the world is the Hyperion Tree, it's location is a secret so you won't be able to see it, but it is about 380 ft. tall.
- Redwood NP and Prairie Creek Redwoods SP are right next to each other, so some of their trails go into both parks or are right on the boundary. The Prairie Creek Redwoods SP area has shorter trails that are easier for children.
- Fern Canyon and Trillium Falls are also must see locations in Prairie Creek Redwoods SP, they are so amazing YouTopo made a travel page in this book just for them under 'Fern Canyon'.

TOP 5 HITS

1. See some of the tallest trees in the park on the Cathedral Trees Trail, 3 mile out and back. (Prairie Creek Redwoods SP)
2. Hike the Revelation Sensory Trail, .25 mile loop. (Prairie Creek Redwoods SP)
3. Find a place to stop, sketch and observe the forest around you.
4. Hike the Lady Bird Johnson Loop, 1.4 mile loop. (Redwoods NP)
5. Keep an eye out for Roosevelt elk at the Elk Meadow. (Prairie Creek Redwoods SP)

Redwood Wonderland

SHOW NOTES

At over 300 feet tall, redwoods are the giants of the forest. These remarkable trees can live to be over 2000 years old—that means some of the trees you pass by were first growing during the time of ancient Rome! Though they are huge and strong, redwoods have shallow root systems, making them vulnerable to being knocked over by strong winds. That's why they grow together in groves, like those of Redwoods National Park.

These groves were in danger in the 1800s, as settlers making their way west cut many down in logging operations. By 1850, roughly 90% of the two million acres of coastal redwoods had been destroyed. The Save the Redwoods League intervened in the 1920s, creating three Northern California state parks: Prairie Creek Redwoods, Jedediah Smith Redwoods, and Del Norte Coast Redwoods. Today, Redwoods National Park works with these state parks to protect the giant trees and the lands around them, including prairies, beaches, and forests.

VIDEOS AND RESOURCES

MY PLAYLIST

music, books, podcasts...

SUGGESTED JAM

Track: Redwood Tree

Artist: Van Morrison

MEET THE LOCALS

get to know the flora, fauna and features

BANANA SLUGS

California banana slugs are the second largest slugs in the world, growing up to nine in long. These slugs are yellow and can have dark spots, making them look like small bananas. They are decomposers, eating everything that is dead (such as fallen leaves, animals, and feces).

SWORD FERN

The sword fern can grow up to four feet tall and lives in cool, shady areas. Its leaves look large and tough compared to other ferns. If you look at the underside of its leaves, you might find orange or yellow spots. These are spores called "sori" that the fern uses to reproduce.

ROOSEVELT ELK

Roosevelt elk are named after Theodore Roosevelt and are the largest elk in North America. They have tan bodies and dark brown necks, with antlers reaching up to four feet long. Female elk are called cows and can be aggressive when protecting their calves.

OCTOPUS TREE

A western hemlock becomes an octopus tree when it grows on a fallen redwood log. As the tree grows upwards, its roots grow all over the log like octopus legs. The hemlock starts its life growing on the log itself. As it gets bigger, it's roots grow around the log in search of soil.

CAT-TAIL MOSS

Cat-tail moss can be found hanging all over the redwood forest. It is a glossy, pale green in color and hangs like hair on tree branches. It is epiphytic, meaning it grows on another plant and depends on it for support but not for food. This moss thrives because of the moisture in the foggy air.

MY REVIEW

Write about your experience

TOP 5 HITS

1. Look for plants and animals in tide pools, .2 mile round trip
2. Rockhound at Agate Beach, .5 mile round trip
3. Search the cliff walls at Agate beach for agates that are becoming exposed by the eroding cliffs.
4. Visit the Sumêg Village and see a reconstruction of a Yurok plank-house village and learn about the Yurok people, .5 mile loop.
5. Hike the Rim Trail, 3.1 miles out and back, for great ocean views.

PRO TIPS

Season: Spring (lowest low tides and least amount of foggy days). Fall will also have less foggy days. Winter is rainy (with about 60 inches of rain a year). Summer has many foggy days.

Difficulty: Easy-moderate, the short hike down to the tidepools has steep stairs cut into the trail that can be slippery.

Time Needed: Day trip

- The tidepools are located at Palmer's Point. Walk down the Palmer's Point Beach Trail down the cliff to the beach to get to the tidepools, .2 mile round trip.
- Tidepools can be very slippery. Wear water shoes that have a grip under them. No flip flops.
- Arrive at tidepools 1 hour before low tide so you can have plenty of time to explore before the tide rises. Gumboot chiton will be found in the grasses. All other creatures will be seen in and near the pools of water in the rocks.
- Bring a flashlight to help identify which rocks are agates at Agate Beach. Agates are transparent so light can pass through them.
- While looking for agates keep an eye on the ocean for rogue waves or sneaker waves. It is not safe to play in the water at Agate Beach.

SHOW NOTES

Long before Europeans reached America, the Yurok people called Sue-meg (Formerly known as Patrick's Point) home. It was here that they fished for salmon in dugout canoes and hunted elk, deer, and birds. By the 1800s, Europeans used the coast of Sue-meg to hunt sea otters for their pelts. The 1850 discovery of gold caused many settlers to move to the area. In order to take the land, these settlers hunted and killed Yurok people and the area underwent environmental devastation from logging and sheep and cattle grazing.

In 1929, the California State Park Commission purchased the land of Sue Meg and in 1990 a crew of Yurok people constructed Sumêg Village from split redwood boards. Tribal members are working to revive their ancient language and traditions. The land at Sue-meg is now cared for and maintained so it resembles its former natural beauty. Today, families can visit the Sue-meg Village, camp, view fascinating tidepools, and rockhound for agates at this exciting state park.

incredible tide pools here

VIDEOS AND RESOURCES

MY PLAYLIST

music, books, podcasts...

SUGGESTED JAM

Track: To California

Artist: The Mighty Mighty Bosstones

MEET THE LOCALS

get to know the flora, fauna and features

GUMBOOT CHITON

The gumboot chiton looks like a large, deflated football on the ground. Its diet of red algae, sea lettuce, and giant kelp help it grow up to 13 inches long. This mollusk moves and grips rocks using its large, muscular foot.

OCHRE SEA STAR

An ochre sea star has five arms and 15,000 tiny appendages called "tube feet" per arm. If it loses an arm, it can grow it back! These creatures throw up one of their two stomachs onto their prey to start digesting their food, then suck the stomach back in to finish eating.

HERMIT CRAB

The hermit crab has a hard exoskeleton on the front of its body and a soft backside. These crustaceans live in borrowed shells to protect themselves. The hermit crab's diet consists of bits of plants and decaying animal matter.

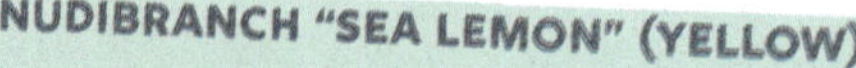

GIANT GREEN PACIFIC ANEMONE

Giant green Pacific anemones are carnivores. They eat crabs, small fish, urchins and mussels. They have tentacles that can paralyze their prey and then bring it to their mouths. They get their green color from micro algae that lives inside it.

NUDIBRANCH "SEA LEMON" (YELLOW)

Nudibranchs are a shell-less mollusk and part of the sea slug family. Their bright colors come from the foods that they eat. Feathery antennae help these creatures to sense food, and feathery gills assist in breathing. Predators spit them out because they smell and taste bad.

MY REVIEW

Write about your experience

PRO TIPS

Season: July - Sept. when it is warm and has the least amount of rain.

Difficulty: Easy

Time Needed: Day trip

- Stay out of the water! Sneaker waves on the beach are dangerous. Do not play in or near the water. People have drowned here.
- Because the waves are so strong, you might see sea stars on the beach. Take a walk and explore. Found seven sea stars on my walk near the rocks on the south side of the beach.
- The drive to Black Sands Beach in Shelter Cove is long and windy. It's worth the drive, but be prepared if anyone gets car sick.
- There are only a few restaurants in Shelter Cove. Most close before eight and don't open every day. Plan ahead of time.
- Shelter Cove is a small town with a small airport and a few restaurants. It is peaceful, beautiful, and very laid back. Plan on a relaxing day trip or a weekend getaway.

TOP 5 HITS

1. Walks on the beach
2. Explore the different coves
3. Picnic and watch the large waves crash against the rocks.
4. Drive to Point Bonita Lighthouse Trail and walk .5 miles to the lighthouse.
5. Watch the sunset

black sands of time

SHOW NOTES

The peaceful, picturesque city of Shelter Cove is home to scenic cliffs and beautiful beaches with black sand. Strong waves mean these beaches are not good for swimming, but they are great for walking, taking pictures, building rock towers, viewing tide pool creatures on nearby rocks, and seeing black sand. This area makes up the southern section of California's 100-mile Lost Coast. This means there are 100 miles of natural, undeveloped coastline that can be hiked and explored.

The sands of Black Sands Beach, one of Shelter Cove's best beaches, is made of a dark sandstone called greywacke and an older, compressed shale produced by tectonic activity. Greywacke is a sedimentary mudstone made from small, mud-like particles (small pieces) containing iron and sandstone that eroded and were carried into the ocean from rivers and settled on the ocean floor.

VIDEOS AND RESOURCES

MY PLAYLIST

music. books. podcasts...

SUGGESTED JAM

Track: California

Artist: Dan Zanes

MEET THE LOCALS

get to know the flora, fauna and features

BLACK SANDS BEACH

CALIFORNIA MUSSEL

The California mussel shuts its shell tightly when it is exposed to air. When it is underwater, it cracks its shell open and releases little cilia (hairs) that will bring in water and food. California mussels glue themselves to rocks by secreting byssal fluid that hardens in sea water.

POISON OAK

Do not touch poison oak. It creates an oil called "urushiol" that causes red rashes, blistering, and itching. Poison oak grows as a shrub and a vine. Its leaves, which turn red during winter, grow in groups of three. You can avoid this plant by remembering the saying "leaves of three, let it be!"

BLACK SAND

Black sand is hidden under all the smooth black rocks covering the beach. The sand is made up of iron rich greywacke and shale, making some of the particles magnetic. These rocks have been weathered into sand by the strong waves that pound on the beach and cliffs.

SEAGULL

Seagulls are white seabirds with dark wingtips, a strong body, and webbed feet. They are intelligent animals that can steal food from other birds, animals and from humans (like a sandwich straight out of kids' unsuspecting hands). They can also drink seawater.

CLIFFS

Black Sands Beach started out as high cliffs. Powerful waves weathered, or broke down, the cliffs over time. As the cliffs weathered, rocks and sediment were deposited at the base of the cliffs, creating the beach. Looking closely and you will see that the rocks in the cliffs are also black.

MY REVIEW

Write about your experience

6

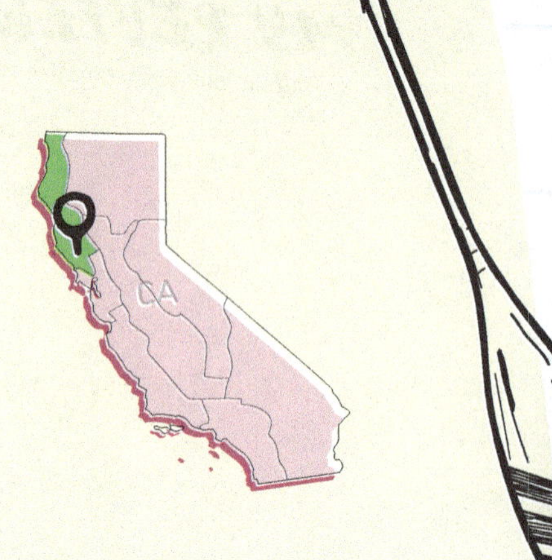

PRO TIPS

Season: Summer and early fall

Difficulty: Easy

Time Needed: 4-6 hours

- Arrive before 10 a.m. to get parking.
- If you have two cars, leave one at Sunset Beach River Park, then drive to Steelhead Beach to get into the water. 2 mile drive.
- If you only have one car, call a ride share to pick you up after your float to drive you back to Steelhead Beach. Cell service can be spotty at Sunset Beach River Park.
- Water and snacks are a must! The float is fun but about 4 hours long. Make stops along the shore to picnic and have snacks.
- You must wear a life jacket. There are life jackets you can borrow at both of the beaches. The water can get between 6 and 20 feet deep. Kids might also want to get out and swim.
- Bring goggles to see the bottom of the river to make your float more enjoyable.
- This river is slow moving. Paddles are helpful but not necessary.
- Reserve your tour at Westside Water Education Center before you go. https://www.sonomawater.org/tours

TOP 5 HITS

1. Tube float, paddleboard, or kayak the river starting at Steelhead Beach and then ending at Sunset Beach River Park.
2. Swim and play in the water at Sunset Beach River Park.
3. Take a free tour at Sonoma County Water Agency, Westside Water Education Center.
4. Relax at the Healdsburg Veterans Memorial Beach.
5. Visit Armstrong Redwoods State Natural Reserve.

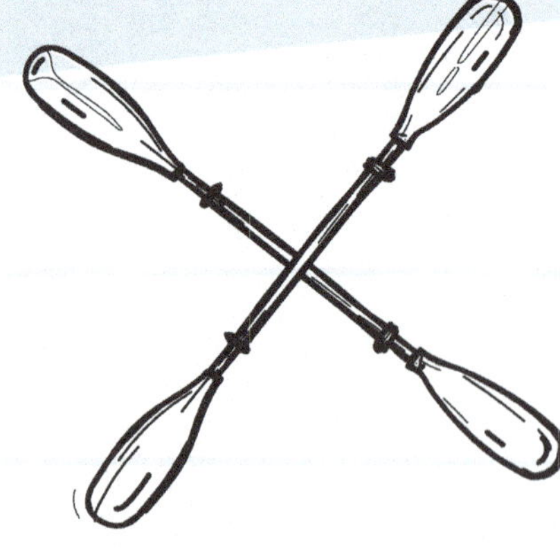

SHOW NOTES

The Russian River has been a source of life for many people for centuries. The Pomo Native Americans inhabited the area as early as 5,000 BCE! Trapping salmon in the river's pools and mining obsidian to make tools, these people lived off the land, river, and ocean. As fur traders made their way to the Russian River, many Pomo were killed by European diseases. Although their numbers have declined, the Pomo people still live in the Russian River Valley today and practice their native traditions.

In the early 19th century, water from the nearby Eel River was diverted to the Potter Valley Hydroelectric Plant that supplied electricity to all of Sonoma, Napa, and Lake Counties. The water was then passed into the Russian River, changing the ecosystem by creating a yearlong water flow. The Russian River supplies drinking water all over Sonoma County.

float on dudes!

VIDEOS AND RESOURCES

MY PLAYLIST

music, books, podcasts...

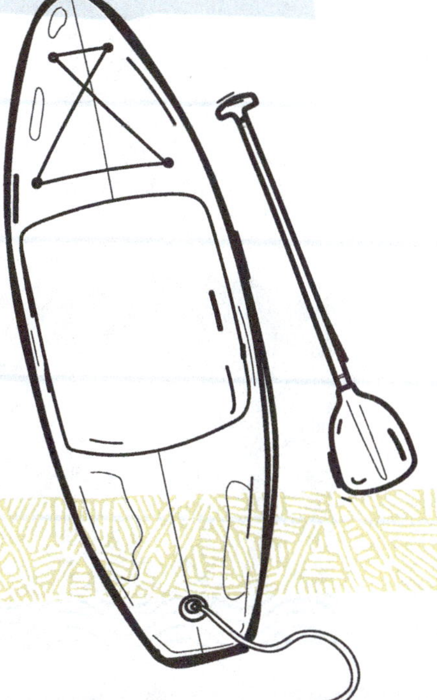

SUGGESTED JAM

Track: Back in California

Artist: Mike Pinto

MEET THE LOCALS

get to know the flora, fauna and features

RUSSIAN RIVER
SUNSET BEACH
RIVER PARK

COMMON MERGANSERS

Female common mergansers have brown heads and necks with shaggy brown crests at the back of their heads. Their bodies are gray with white at the base of their neck. These birds dive deep into the water to catch fish to eat. They live in tree cavities near rivers and lakes.

GREAT EGRET

Great egrets have black legs, long yellow beaks, and white feathers. They can often be seen standing perfectly still while hunting in shallow water. When a frog or fish gets close, they quickly jab their beaks into the water to catch them.

PEREGRINE FALCON

Flying up to speeds of 200 miles per hour, this is the fastest animal on the planet! The fastest recorded peregrine falcon flight is clocked at 242 miles per hour. These birds are carnivores, hunting other birds and catching them mid-flight.

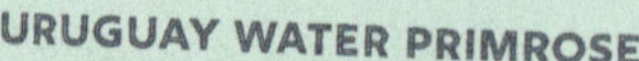

BLACK-CROWNED NIGHT HERON

The black-crowned night heron is a short, compact heron that often tucks its head down into its body, giving it a hunchback appearance. It lives near rivers, estuaries, and marshes so that it can hunt its underwater prey: fish, squid, frogs, clams, and crustaceans.

URUGUAY WATER PRIMROSE

The Uruguay water primrose is an invasive species that forms dense, green mats over the water and thick stalks under it. It slows down the movement of water, destroys the habitat of fish and birds, and stops the growth of native plants.

MY REVIEW

Write about your experience

SHASTA CASCADES & MODOC PLATEAU

This northern region of California is an amazing mix of volcanic peaks, underground caves, cascading waterfalls, and dry rugged landscapes. Get tubular exploring underground lava tubes at Lava Beds National Monument or go big and see the expansive limestone caves of Shasta Cavern with their impressive stalactites, stalagmites, draperies, columns and other formations that have been 250 million years in the making! At Burney Falls you can get up and personal in what might be the most unique waterfall in the state. Take a dip in the McCloud River where you'll find 3 beautiful and impressive cascading falls. Interested in places with names like Bumpass Hell or Devils Kitchen? Then you absolutely must check out the geothermal wonderland of Lassen Volcanic National Park where you can see boiling mud pots, sulfur works, pristine lakes, cascading waterfalls, and beautiful meadows.

PRO TIPS

Season: Open year round, but open for longer hours in the summer.

Difficulty: Easy- moderate, some caves require crouching down.

Time Needed: 2-3 days

- You can buy a book of cave maps to help you navigate the inside of the caves in the Visitor Center.
- The Visitor Center has flashlights for you to borrow, bring your own just in case they run out.
- A bike helmet is good enough to wear into the caves.
- Bring a jacket, the cave temperature is about 55 degrees F year round.
- Parking for about 2-4 cars is available near each cave entrance.
- Bonus adventure: visit Little Glass Mountain is 40.6 miles from Lava Beds. This lava flow is only 1000 years old and offers up to 4.6 miles of trails through large piles of obsidian. It is completely surrounded by lush green forest so prepare to be astounded by the first glimpses of the flow as you get close.

TOP 5 HITS

1. Explore the lava tubes around Cave Loop and visit Skull Cave.
2. See ancient art at Big Painted Cave and Symbol Bridge 1.6 miles out and back.
3. Hike to see Mammoth Crater, .1 mile.
4. Visit the Modoc War historical site, Captain Jack's Stronghold, choice of .5 mile or 1.5 mile trail. (learning pamphlet available in Visitor Center)
5. Visit Petroglyph Point.

skull cave!

SHOW NOTES

If you could rewind a century and a half, you would see a much different place than what you see today at Lava Beds. In 1872, it was the site of a conflict called the Modoc War. The Modoc people, American Indians from Oregon, were forced off their ancestral lands so that settlers could take them and they were moved to reservations with bad conditions. They eventually fought back. Through strategy and use of the cave systems at Lava Beds, fewer than 60 Modoc warriors were able to hold back a force of up to 600 US soldiers for months before eventually being captured.

The area's geological past is even more violent. Lava Beds is shaped by the nearby Medicine Lake Volcano, the largest volcano in the Cascade Range. This volcano has erupted numerous times--here at Lava Beds, you can see evidence of over 30 separate lava flows. These lava flows hardened as they cooled and produced the rocks all around you, as well as the iconic lava tube caves that stretch through the area.

VIDEOS AND RESOURCES

MY PLAYLIST

music, books, podcasts...

SUGGESTED JAM

Track: California I'm Comin

Artist: Little Richard Band

MEET THE LOCALS

get to know the flora, fauna and features

HYDROPHOBIC BACTERIA

Golden Dome at Lava Beds National Monument is home to a very special microorganism. Look up in this cave and you might think the ceiling has been painted gold. This metallic sparkle is caused by colonies of hydrophobic bacteria. Do not touch! One fingerprint could take about 40 years to heal.

PETROGLYPH POINT

Petroglyph Point is the largest rock art site in North America, with over 5000 symbols carved into it. These carvings were made by artists in canoes, who carved by making holes and connecting them. Their meaning is unknown. Look around and see what meaning they might have for you.

LAVA FLOW

Medicine Lake Shield Volcano has a 7.46 by 4.35 mile shallow crater (caldera). The Devils Homestead Flow came from Fleener Chimneys 2000-8000 years ago. It is one of over 520 surface vents on the Medicine Lake Shield Volcano that magma has erupted or flowed from.

LAVACICLE

Lavacicles are created when lava drips from the ceiling. As the tube cools, it makes a stalactite structure that looks like an icicle. Lavacicles can be as long as six feet, but the ones at Lava Beds tend to be smaller. Their dark shine makes them look as if they were covered in melted chocolate!

WYOMING INDIAN PAINTBRUSH

The Wyoming Indian paintbrush is named for its vivid red coloration--it looks like it was dipped upside down in red paint! These red parts may look like flowers, but they're actually modified leaves. Indian paintbrushes survive by stealing nutrients from the roots of other plants.

MY REVIEW

Write about your experience

8

BURNEY FALLS

MCARTHUR-BURNEY FALLS MEMORIAL STATE PARK

DATE ______________

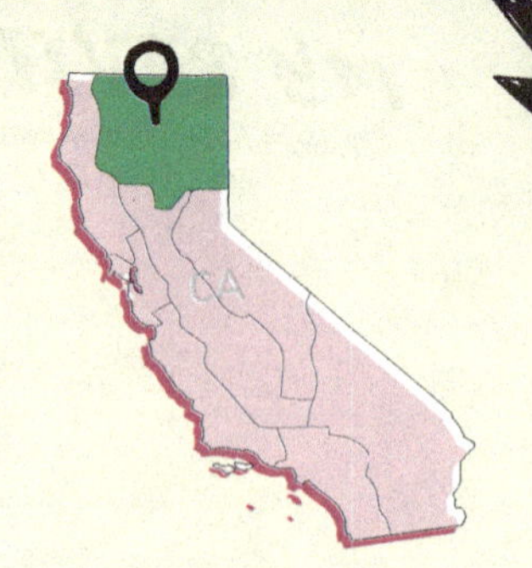

PRO TIPS

Season: Spring and summer

Difficulty: Easy

Time Needed: 1 day

- The lower, middle, and upper falls on the McCloud River all have parking lots.
- You can hike from McCloud River Lower Falls to both middle and upper falls, or you can take a short drive and park near each waterfall.
- The water of the McCloud River is cold but feels refreshing on a hot day.
- The swim holes are located at McCloud Lower Falls just above the falls.
- When visiting Burney Falls hike to the pool at the base of the falls, sit on the rocks and feel the mist. Do not swim here.
- You can walk down to the base of Burney Falls and then back up if you don't want to hike the 1 mile loop. The walkway down to the falls and the falls overlook is right next to the parking lot.

TOP FIVE HITS

1. Hike to the bottom of Burney Falls, 1 mile loop, and feel it's spray.
2. Hike or drive to the McCloud River Lower, Middle, and Upper Falls, 3.5 mile hike, out and back trail.
3. Swim in the pools above the McCloud Lower Falls (warm weather only)
4. Play in the river next to McCloud Upper Falls parking.
5. Watch for wildlife at McCloud Upper Falls.

Weekend at Burney Falls!

VIDEOS AND RESOURCES

MY PLAYLIST

SHOW NOTES

McArthur-Burney Falls Memorial State Park and the McCloud River feature several stunning waterfalls. As you explore them, you might notice canyons of basalt, a rock formed from cooled lava. In some places, this rock even forms into hexagonal columns. The McCloud River and Burney Creek constantly pound against this rock, and even though rock may sometimes seem stronger than water, the canyons here are proof that the water is winning. The river's power may be most apparent when watching the area's waterfalls. Burney Falls, for example, is 129 feet tall, with 100 million gallons of water passing through it every single day.

Throughout time, humans have learned to channel this pressure to perform tasks it would be very difficult for a human to do. In modern times, this includes converting the energy of water into electrical energy. The McCloud River Dam does exactly this, with a generating capacity of 364 megawatts of energy (enough to power nearly 200,000 homes).

SUGGESTED JAM

Track: Back to California

Artist: Carole King

MEET THE LOCALS

get to know the flora, fauna and features

INDIAN RHUBARB

Indian rhubarb is known as the "umbrella plant", and when you see one, you'll understand why. This plant's leaves can grow up to two feet across! A stem that attaches to the center of the leaf creates a dimple that catches water, allowing this plant to store it for later use.

PONDEROSA PINE

To identify a ponderosa pine, look for tall, straight trunks with rusty orange bark. Hanging from this pine in bunches of three are four to eight-inch needles. The most interesting feature that gives this tree away, though, is its scent--ponderosa bark smells like vanilla!

COLUMBIAN BLACK-TAILED DEER

The Columbian black-tailed deer isn't its own species, but rather a subspecies of the mule deer. Unlike their mule deer cousins, these deer have--you guessed it!--a black tail. Black-tailed deer babies (fawns) are born completely without scent to keep hidden from predators.

BASALT

The top lip of Burney Falls is made of basalt, a volcanic igneous rock that was formed about 200,000 years ago. This type of rock is not only important in the formation of the planet Earth, but it also makes up a large portion of the moon!

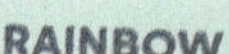

RAINBOW

Rainbows are formed when water in the air reflects the colors traveling through in light. This can often happen in the mists surrounding waterfalls. Make sure the sun is behind you to help you find a rainbow in this mist, and try and spot your favorite color!

MY REVIEW ☆☆☆☆☆

Write about your experience

9

DATE

LAKE SHASTA CAVERNS

NATIONAL NATURAL LANDMARK

PRO TIPS

Season: Open year round

Difficulty: Easy-moderate (lots of wet steps)

Time Needed: 2-3 hours

- Food and drinks are not allowed in the cave.
- Just getting to the cave is an adventure. You will ride a boat across the lake, followed by a bus ride up a windy road up to the cave entrance!
- Take your time and encourage kids to ask a lot of questions to your guide.
- Actively search for the cave formations with food names, turn it into a game to earn a cave party.
- A cave party is where you celebrate your trip by making all the foods that sound like cave formations you saw in the cave. (Bacon, popcorn, grapes, soda "soda straws", cauliflower etc.)
- Ask your tour guide to help you find different cave formations.
- Tours of Shasta Dam are free and take one hour. Call for times and reservations.

TOP 5 HITS

1. Take the guided Lake Shasta Caverns tour.
2. Enjoy the boat ride across the McCloud Arm of Shasta Lake.
3. Look for stalactites, stalagmites, little brown bats and cave bacon.
4. Visit Shasta Dam, take a free tour, and take in the sites.
5. Have a cave party, eat all the foods that the cave formations you saw were named after! (Bacon, popcorn, soda "soda straws", cauliflower etc.)

Behold the grandeur

SHOW NOTES

When you enter the Lake Shasta Caverns, you are entering geological prehistory. Around the time dinosaurs first started roaming the supercontinent of Pangaea, this cave began to form. Limestone caverns like this one are created when rain combines with carbon dioxide in the atmosphere. This transforms the water into a weak acid. When this acidic rainwater finds its way into porous limestone (through groundwater or underground rivers), it gradually dissolves the rock. In some cases, it dissolves enough rock to create bigger holes, which after thousands of years can become caves. This process creates incredible formations such as stalactites (icicle-like rocks hanging from the cave ceiling), stalagmites (columns growing from the floor), hollow rock straws, and even curtains that look like bacon!

If you find caves intriguing, you're not alone—caves have fascinated humans for thousands of years. Prehistoric people used caves for shelter and, in some places in the world, left beautiful and elaborate art inside of them. Members of the Wintu Tribe were likely aware of Lake Shasta Caverns for centuries. Europeans discovered them in the late 1800s and used ropes, ladders, and lanterns to explore.

VIDEOS AND RESOURCES

MY PLAYLIST

SUGGESTED JAM

Track: California Blue

Artist: Roy Orbison

MEET THE LOCALS

get to know the flora, fauna and features

STALACTITES

These structures, which are shaped like icicles hanging from cave ceilings, are created when water containing dissolved minerals drips from the top of the cave, leaving tiny bits of these minerals behind. You can remember what a stalactite looks like by remembering that it holds tight to the cave ceiling.

STALAGMITES

Though stalagmites appear to be growing up from the ground, they actually are the result of water dripping from the ceiling. This water leaves small amounts of minerals where it drops, which build up slowly after thousands of years to produce a stalagmite.

SODA STRAWS

Just like the straws you might use at a restaurant, soda straw cave formations are stalactites developed in the shape of hollow tubes. As cave water drips through these tubes, it leaves a tiny rim of deposited mineral at the bottom of the soda straw, helping it grow longer.

COLUMN

When a stalactite hanging from the cave ceiling and a stalagmite rising from the cave floor meet, they create a formation called a column. Columns can also be created when a stalactite reaches all the way to the bottom of a cave. In both cases, this can take thousands to millions of years.

CAVE BACON

Cave bacon is a special type of flowstone that looks just like a piece of the mouthwatering bacon. The layered appearance of cave bacon shows times in geological history where the flow of the water in the cave changed--perhaps there was less rain, or different amounts of minerals in the water.

MY REVIEW

Write about your experience

10

LASSEN VOLCANIC

DATE

NATIONAL PARK

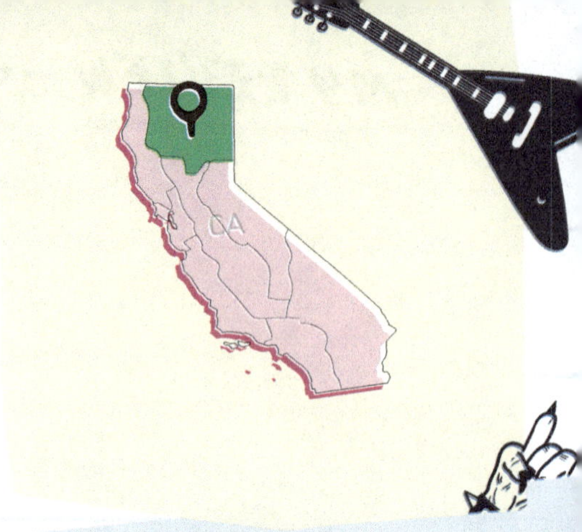

PRO TIPS

Season: July -Oct., summer-early fall

Difficulty: Easy- moderate hikes

Time Needed: 3-4 days to see the whole park

- If possible, break up your trip into three different days for the three different sections of the park. (Cinder Cone/Butte Lake area, Devils Kitchen area, and Mt Lassen/ Bumpass Hell/ Kings Creek area
- The roads to see Lassen Volcanic National Park are designed around the outside of the park. There is not a road inside Lassen with access to all parts of the park.
- The Bumpass Hell area does not open until all the snow melts from the trail, which can take until early July. Call to check status at 530-595-4480.
- Camp as close to the park as possible. The drives to the different areas of the park can be long (one to two hours).
- Restrooms for Devils Kitchen are located at the camping area further up the road from the parking lot on the right hand side.
- The most visited area of the park is the Mt Lassen/ Bumpass Hell/ Kings Creek area.
- After seeing Kings Creek Falls follow the trail up river to see the Cascades Waterfall section just above the main falls.
- Stop at the Devastated Area to see the destruction of Mt. Lassen's last eruption. .5 mile loop trail.

TOP 5 HITS

1. Hike the Bumpass Hell Trail, 2.7 miles out and back. (check if it's open before going)
2. Explore the waterfalls of Kings Creek, 2.3 miles out and back.
3. See fumaroles and mud pots at Sulphur Works, located right next to the parking lot.
4. Hike through lush meadows and forest to Devils Kitchen, 4.2 mile out and back.
5. Experience a volcano crater at the Cinder Cone Trail, 1.5 miles with 850 ft. elevation gain.

SHOW NOTES

Lassen Volcanic National Park has a diverse landscape of boiling springs, steaming fumaroles, mud pots, clear mountain lakes, waterfalls, lush meadows and volcanoes. Unknown to many, It has the second largest hydrothermal area in the USA, called Bumpass Hell. Bumpass Hell has boiling springs, bubbling mud pots, hissing steam vents, and roaring fumaroles, all of which can be admired from safe, man-made boardwalks.

The park has all four different types of volcanoes: a plug dome (Lassen Peak), a cinder cone (Cinder Cone), a composite volcano (Brokeoff Volcano), and a shield volcano (Prospect Peak). Mount Lassen is the southernmost active volcano in the Cascade Range. It had its last major eruption in 1914 and smaller eruptions through 1917. Rocks and boulders were thrown over 3.7 miles away from the volcanic eruption. Three days after the eruption, Benjamin Franklin Loomis took photographs that brought national attention to Mount Lassen and helped to bring about the establishment of Lassen Volcanic National Park. You can go and see this eruption site, known as the Devastated Area.

Bumpass Hell

VIDEOS AND RESOURCES

MY PLAYLIST

music, books, podcasts...

SUGGESTED JAM

Track: Northern California Girls

Artist: Camper Van Beethoven

MEET THE LOCALS

get to know the flora, fauna and features

LASSEN VOLCANIC NATIONAL PARK

MUDPOT

A mudpot is an acidic hot spring. It forms where magma is close to the earth's surface. Water sinks into the ground, is heated, and rises as steam. This steam heats a small amount of surface water that mixes with soil rich in volcanic ash, forming acidic boiling mud!

FUMAROLE

A fumarole is a vent or crack in the earth through which gas and steam rises. It forms when water sinks into the ground and reaches a magma chamber near the surface. This water is heated and turned into steam that rises with other volcanic gas through vents in the earth crust.

THERMOPHILIC BACTERIA

Thermophilic bacteria are heat-loving microorganisms that live in hot springs. Different colors depend on the spring's temperature. Blue, green, and brown love water up to 167 degrees Fahrenheit. Orange and rust-colored bacteria prefer "cooler" hot water.

CORN LILY

These lilies love moist meadows and riverbeds at high elevations. Their many white flowers are highly toxic, making them harmful to all animals that try to eat them. Native Americans used corn lily leaves to poison arrowheads.

WOLF LICHEN

Wolf lichen is a yellow-green, moss-like lichen that grows in clumps on tree bark. Its bright color comes from the poisonous vulpina acid inside it. This acid gives the plant its name--it was historically ground down and added to meat to poison wolves and foxes.

MY REVIEW

Write about your experience

BAY AREA

Escape the concrete jungle and get lost in some amazing outdoor destinations of the Bay Area. Head to Point Reyes National Seashore and you can witness the California native Tule Elk, visit a Miwok (not Ewok) village, hike the bluffs, or relax on the beach. Muir Woods National Monument will inspire and uplift you as you look up to the redwood giants or look down at your feet to find an assortment of mushrooms. Get a new perspective of the Golden Gate Bridge as you meander through the trails at Lands End as it opens and closes to a changing view of the great bridge. The Bay Area also has some great beaches. One of our favorites is Natural Bridges State Beach where you can watch the surf crash into the keyhole rock, explore the rock tide pools,or possibly encounter a monarch butterfly migration.

PRO TIPS

Season: Fall, winter and spring. Summer brings clouds and lots of fog.

Difficulty: Easy-moderate, trail near cliffs.

Time Needed: 1-2 Days

- Estero hike is an easy mellow hike,on a 2-3 people wide trail. There is lots of poison oak to the side of the trail. The bridge is a great place for shorebird viewing and crabs can be found on the rocks under the bridge. Recommend turning around after the bridge.
- The Elk reserve is worth the visit. Hike along the Tomales Point Trail to see herds of Tule Elk and cliff ocean views. Be prepared for a long drive through barren dairy farm land to get to it.
- Don't walk on the mudflats, they are delicate habitats and it's dangerous, you can sink deep into the mud.
- Cypress Tree Tunnel is off the main road on the way to Drakes Beach, it's a fun place for pictures.
- If you want to kayak the area with kids go to Whitehouse Pool near Point Reyes Station. There is a parking lot and a place to kayak or paddleboard the Tomales Bay Ecological Preserve.
- The Miwok Lolo Village is a replica of early Miwok Native American homes in Point Reyes.

TOP 5 HITS

1. Hike Tomales Point Trail, 4 miles round trip.
2. Hike the Estero Trail to the footbridge, 2.4 miles round trip.
3. Walk Kule Loklo Trail, .8 mile, to the Miwok Lolo Village.
4. Check out Point Reyes Lighthouse, 0.7 walk.
5. Relax at Drakes Beach and swim or wet your feet.

SHOW NOTES

At over 300 feet tall, redwoods are the giants of the forest. These remarkable trees can live to be over 2000 years old--that means some of the trees you pass by were first growing during the time of ancient Rome! Though they are huge and strong, redwoods have shallow root systems, making them vulnerable to being knocked over by strong winds. That's why they grow together in groves, like those of Redwoods National Park.

These groves were in danger in the 1800s, as settlers making their way west cut many down in logging operations. By 1850, roughly 90% of the two million acres of coastal redwoods had been destroyed. The Save the Redwoods League intervened in the 1920s, creating three Northern California state parks: Prairie Creek Redwoods, Jedediah Smith Redwoods, and Del Norte Coast Redwoods. Today, Redwoods National Park works with these state parks to protect the giant trees and the lands around them, including prairies, beaches, and forests.

lighthouse

VIDEOS AND RESOURCES

MY PLAYLIST

music, books, podcasts...

SUGGESTED JAM

Track: California English Pt 2.

Artist: Vampire Weekend

MEET THE LOCALS

get to know the flora, fauna and features

POINT REYES

MONTEREY CYPRESS TREE

The Monterey cypress can live in harsh, windy, salty, coastal areas where other plants can't survive. Ocean winds sculpt the tree into unique picturesque shapes. It is an evergreen tree and produces small ¼ in. male and 1 in. female cones on the same tree.

TULE ELK

Tule elk are an endemic species to California, where today they number around 5,700 animals. This number is less than the historic population, numbering 500,000. Males may weigh up to 700 pounds, while antlerless females may weigh upwards of 400 pounds.

TURKEY VULTURE

Turkey vultures are scavengers that don't kill their own prey. They use their powerful beak to help force their heads into the body of dead animals. With the ability to identify scents over a mile away, these animals possess the strongest sense of smell of all birds.

MIWOK LOKLO VILLAGE

The coastal Miwok people lived in the area of Point Reyes where they were successful as a gathering, fishing and hunting community. Visitors can explore Kule Loklo, which means Bear Valley, a re-created village that closely resembles that of the native Miwok people.

EUCALYPTUS SEEDS

Eucalyptus seeds are contained in small acorn-resembling pods. Both red gum and blue gum species reproduce throughout California via seeds that range in color from brown or black to orange or tan. Eucalyptus plants are native to Australia but thrive in the California environment.

MY REVIEW ☆☆☆☆☆

Write about your experience

PRO TIPS

Season: Oct.- May, for less crowds

Difficulty: Easy-moderate, Some steps and uphill hiking.

Time Needed: Day trip

- You need to get a Parking Reservation before you visit.
- There is a shuttle service on the weekends for $3.50 ages 16-adult and free for ages 15 and under, park at 100 Shoreline Hwy, Mill Valley, CA 94941
- Download directions to Muir Woods and directions from Muir Woods to the beach BEFORE you go. There is no cell service at Muir Woods so you will pass the beach as you leave the woods if you don't know where you are going.
- The Redwood Trail is an ADA accessible wide boardwalk that follows Redwood Creek. You can walk this loop trail on both sides of the river. Also look for Steelhead Trout swimming up Redwood Creek.
- Take the Canopy View Trail to Lost Creek Trail to Fern Creek Trail for a fun kid friendly loop. Canopy View trail is uphill, Lost Creek Trail takes you back down hill then Fern Creek Trail is flat. At the end of the Fern Trail Creek Trail walk the Redwood Creek Trail to the park entrance. Full Loop to the park entrance is about 4 miles.

TOP 5 HITS

1. Canopy View Trail to Lost Creek Trail to Fern Creek Trail Loop, 3 mile loop.
2. Take pictures at the metal bridge on the Fern Creek Trail.
3. Redwood Trail, 2 miles round trip.
4. Play at Muir beach.
5. Muir Beach overlook - .1 mile short trail overlooking the beach and coast.

- The Redwood Trail is the busiest trail and connects you with all the other trails. Take the side trails such as the Canopy View trail to get away from the crowds.
- Take the Canopy View Trail to the top to see the view above the trees before heading back down the lost trail.
- Fern Creek Trail is a flat trail with lush green ferns, trees and a large metal bridge. The bridge is located where the trail connects to the Lost Trail. It's a great spot to touch the water, have a snack or take a family picture.
- Muir Woods can be done in the morning leaving the early afternoon open for playing Muir Beach. This is a beautiful black sand beach next to wetlands.
- Visit the Muir Beach Overlook at sunset to finish your day.

SHOW NOTE

Muir Woods National Monument was the first National Monument to be created after its 295 acres of land was donated to the United States. Congressman Willaim Kent donated the land in order to protect the redwoods from the logging industry. About 1 year before Muir Woods became a National Monument 80% of the City of San Francisco had burned down and the people were needing to rebuild. By donating the land of Muir Woods, the tallest trees in the world were preserved for future generations.

Today Muir Woods is a treasured escape from the hustle and bustle of the big city. This area is so pristine that not even cell phones can penetrate the beauty and peace of this redwood forest. This is a place where you can immerse yourself in the sounds, sites, and smells of the ferns, creeks, large redwoods and colors of the forest. You can experience salmon and trout swimming up river, and enjoy the luscious green ferns and mosses that cover the ground and trees making it a wonderland of green.

VIDEOS AND RESOURCES

Muir Woods

MY PLAYLIST

music, books, podcasts...

SUGGESTED JAM

Track: San Francisco

Artist: The Mowgli's

MEET THE LOCALS

get to know the flora, fauna and features

REDWOOD SORREL

Redwoods love shade and have edible, clover-shaped leaves (0.4 to two inches long). These leaves have a tangy, lemony flavor but are mildly toxic, so they should only be eaten in small quantities. Native American tribes still use this plant as a garnish for dried fish and as a type of medicine.

WESTERN SWORD FERN

The sword fern can grow up to four feet tall and grow in cool shady areas. Its leaves look large and tough compared to other ferns. If you look at the underside of its leaves you might find orange or yellow spots. These are spores called "sori" that the fern uses to reproduce.

WILD TURKEY

Wild turkeys can fly in short bursts and sleep in trees. A group of turkeys is called a flock. Male and female turkeys have different shaped poop. The female's poop is spiral shaped and the male's poop is long and J shaped. The reddish flap of skin under its chin is called a wattle.

CALIFORNIA BAY LAUREL TREE

The leaves of the California bay laurel tree can be used fresh or dried in cooking soups and sauces. They have also been used as bug repellent, as a way to get rid of lice, and to help with headaches or colds. In Greece winners of poetry and athletic contests wore crowns made of bay laurels.

REDWOOD BURL

A redwood burl is a knobby looking growth on the tree. These growths are home to redwood bud tissue. If a tree were to fall this bud tissue can grow into a genetic clone or replica of the fallen tree! This is one of two ways that redwoods reproduce: from seeds or from burls.

MY REVIEW

Write about your experience

13

DATE

GOLDEN GATE NATIONAL RECREATION AREA

PRO TIPS

Season: Fall, spring, and winter, the summer can be really foggy

Difficulty: Easy scenic hike

Time Needed: Half day

- The Lands End Coastal Trail can be hiked out and back or in a loop if you follow the El Camino Del Mar Trail back to the parking lot. The distance is about the same.
- Visit Mile Rock Beach at low tide, it disappears at high tide.
- You can take dogs on a leash to hike the trails.
- Bathrooms are located in parking lot areas only.
- This is a high use trail so expect long lines for the bathrooms and lots of people hiking.
- Search for the heart rock formation from the Point Lobos Overlook.
- The Labyrinth is located at Lands End Point near One Mile Beach.
- This is a coastal trail and can get windy, so bring a jacket.

1. Hike the Lands End Coastal Trail, 2.6 mile out and back.
2. Visit the ruins of Sutro Baths then walk into the cave next to Sutro Baths. Watch the powerful waves crash into the rocks. Short downhill walk from the main parking.
3. Hike down to see the Labyrinth .4 mile round trip off of the Lands End Trail.
4. View tidepools at Mile Rock Beach at low tide, this hiking distance is included in the .4 mile round trip Labyrinth hike.
5. Take in the view of the Golden Gate Bridge from Eagles Point Overlook.

Views of Golden Gate Bridge!

SHOW NOTES

The Land's End National Recreational Center is within the center of a lively historical landscape. When the Spanish explorers looked out over the land, they named this spot "Point Lobos," for the many lobos marinos (which means sea lions) that were on the offshore rocks. Visitors can still see shipwrecks at low tide, World War II Cruisers, and the ruins of Sutro Baths that highlight this area's diverse history. Today, the area has winding trails that provide overlooks of the San Francisco coastline, rocky cliffs, shady shrubbery and the Golden Gate Bridge.

Walking the Coastal Trail allows you to be on the very edge of the continent! This vantage point gives visitors the opportunity to look for migrating whales, which could be moving through at any time of year since different species move at varying times. From Point Lobos, Ocean Beach, or Fort Funston Beach, keep an eye out for large humpback whales (reaching up to 50-feet long) breaching and spouting from May to November. Gray whales and orcas may move through the area in winter and spring, and blue whales move through beginning in July.

VIDEOS AND RESOURCES

MY PLAYLIST

music, books, podcasts...

SUGGESTED JAM

Track: San Francisco

Track: Foxygen

MEET THE LOCALS

get to know the flora, fauna and features

MILE ROCK LIGHTHOUSE

Mile Rock Lighthouse was built to warn ships of the hazardous rocks and tides in the area. Several ships had shipwrecked in the area and hundreds of lives were lost. It served as a lighthouse for about 60 years then was turned into a helicopter landing pad in the 1960's.

GOLDEN GATE BRIDGE

The Golden Gate Bridge got its name because it crosses the Golden Gate Strait. A strait is a narrow body of water that connects two larger bodies of water. It is a suspension bridge meaning; vertical suspender towers and cables are used to hold up the road.

HEART SHAPED ROCK

The heart-shaped rock can be seen at the Point Lobos Lookout. It has slowly been shaped by the constant pounding of the ocean waves. Look closely because the heart is hidden. You can only see it if you look at it from the right angle.

THE LABYRINTH

The Labyrinth was created by artist Eduardo Aguilera as a shrine to "peace, love and enlightenment." It has been at Lands End for almost 20 years and in that time it was destroyed twice. Each time Aguilera returned and rebuilt it. Please look but don't touch.

SUTRO BATHS

Sutro Baths was once the world's largest indoor swimming facility, with seven different temperature pools to choose from. A series of concrete tunnels and tanks used the force of the tides to fill up the pools. 10,000 people could visit at the same time.

MY REVIEW

Write about your experience

14

NATURAL BRIDGES STATE BEACH

DATE HERE

CALIFORNIA

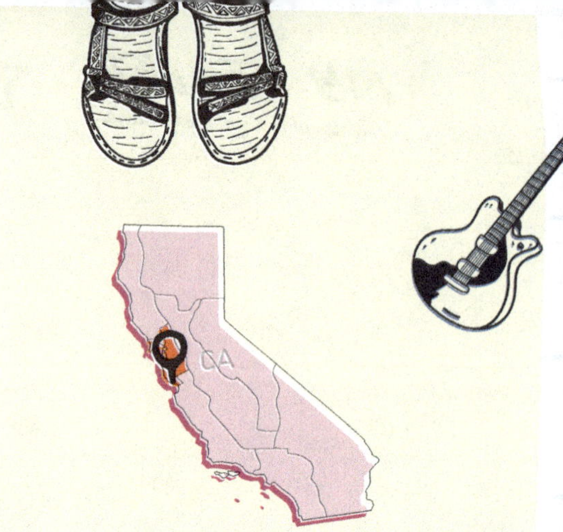

PRO TIPS

Season: Year round

Difficulty: Easy-moderate, tide pool rocks slippery when wet.

Time Needed: Day trip

- The best tide pools are on the second rock shelf area west of the beach.
- Be aware of the ocean and tides. As the tide rises these tide pools can become dangerous.
- Keep kids away from the rock edges. These tide pools are on a rock shelf raised higher than the beach.
- Reserve volunteers can be found at the tide pools, they can help you find and identify tide pool animals and plants.
- Monarch butterflies populations are declining, check out https://www.saveourmonarchs.org/ to see how your family can help butterflies.

TOP 5 HITS

1. Explore and view tide pools and tide pools animals.
2. Take pictures near the natural bridge rock formation.
3. Picnic and play on the beach.
4. View monarch butterflies in the Monarch Grove late Oct.- Late Jan.
5. Take a walk through Moore Creek Wetlands Preserve.

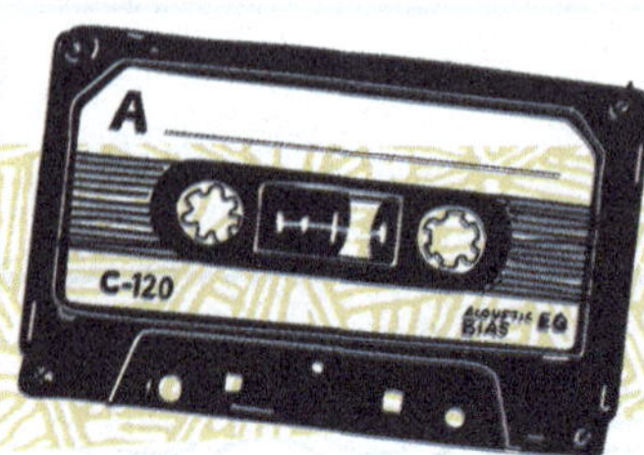

SHOW NOTES

This protected stretch of beach has some of the best tide pools to explore in the whole country! When the tide retreats each day, visitors gain access to pools full of vibrant life, ranging from sea anemones, snails, sea stars, shore crabs, kelp, and more. In every 24-hour stretch, there are two high tides and two low tides, pulled by the earth's rotational force and the gravity of the moon.

Looking out from shore, visitors may catch glimpses of active seabirds diving and bobbing for food, or see a spout of air from a migrating whale's blowhole, or witness playful seals and otters going about their daily activities. Hiking through the Moore Creek Wetlands Preserve is a great place to look for amphibians, birds, and other creatures among the freshwater wetlands and salt marshes. In the early spring, the surrounding shrublands and grasslands are alive with buzzing pollinators and brightly colored wildflowers. The Monarch Butterfly Natural Preserve here is an excellent area to observe migrating monarchs from October to January, when they gather in groups numbering in the thousands.

rockin' bridges

MY PLAYLIST

music, books, podcasts...

VIDEOS AND RESOURCES

SUGGESTED JAM

Track: Santa Cruz (You're not that far)

Artist: The Thrills

MEET THE LOCALS

get to know the flora, fauna and features

PACIFIC PURPLE SEA URCHIN

Pacific purple sea urchins are a bright purple color and are covered in pincers, tube feet and purple spines. They use their spines for protection and to grab food and move it towards their mouth. If the water gets warmer than 79 degrees; it will kill them.

GIANT GREEN PACIFIC ANEMONE

Giant green Pacific anemones are carnivores. They eat crabs, small fish, urchins and mussels. They have tentacles that can paralyze their prey and then bring it to their mouths. They get their green color from micro algae that lives inside it.

PERIWINKLE

A periwinkle is a sea snail that lives on intertidal rocks. It grows its own shell that it uses for protection. It uses its radula "file-like tongue" to eat algae on rocks and diatoms (phytoplankton) in the water. When it dies a hermit crab will move into its shell.

CHITON

Chiton is a flattened symmetrical marine mollusk. They have eight valves or plates on their mantle that can shift and move as the animal moves. They also have a powerful foot that can hold onto rocks. They are hard to remove from rocks!

GOOSENECK BARNACLE

Gooseneck barnacles have a long fleshy stem that looks like a neck and live attached to rocks and flotsam. Above their stems they grow many plates around their body for protection. When it is underwater it uses its feathery feet that they use to filter feed and breath.

MY REVIEW ☆☆☆☆☆

Write about your experience

CENTRAL COAST

The Central Coast of California is an amazing extent of rugged coastline that is accessible to both the Bay Area and Southern California. It includes Channel Islands National Park with its extensive sea caves, extremely curious island fox, and other endemic plant life only found on this island. Stroll purple sand beaches, hike to see a tidefall (waterfall on the beach) of McWay Falls, or take a redwood hike off the famous coastline known as Big Sur. Get a closer look of sea creatures at the world class aquarium in Monterey Bay (you will be completely blown away by the Giant Pacific Octopus) or behold the larger than life Elephant Seals as they fight, mate, and give birth at the Elephant Seal Vista Point found in San Simeon. It's a sight you won't forget. Head inland and you can explore the Talus Caves and rocky peaks of Pinnacles National Park where you just might spot the iconic California Condor flying overhead. You can also scramble and boulder your way around Lizards Mouth Rock where you'll get a stunning view of the charming city of Santa Barbara.

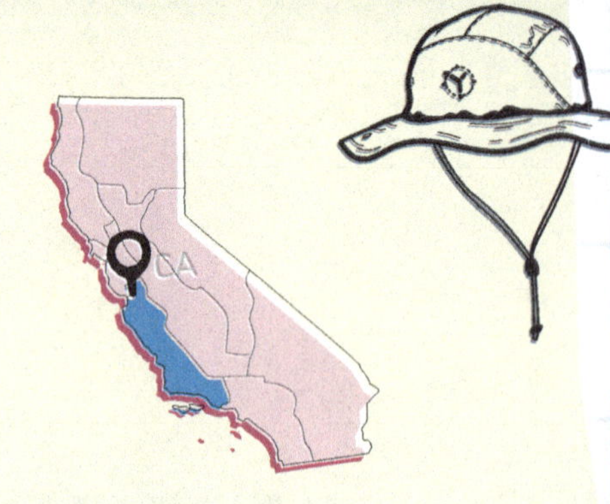

PRO TIPS

Season: Year round, Wed.-Sun. 9 a.m.-5 p.m.

Difficulty: Easy-moderate trails, with three main routes to choose from.

Time Needed: 2-3 hours minimum to hike and explore. Closed Mon. and Tues.

- Bring binoculars to see the many different birds and animals. Take time to observe and sketch them.
- All visitors should check-in at the Visitor's Center, which also serves as the area's trailhead. Pets and bicycles are prohibited.
- The trail towards Big Barn, has owl boxes and is the fastest route to the water.
- Listen and find woodpeckers in the oak woodland area of the south marsh loop.
- Elkhorn Slough hosts active research plots. Observe from a distance and be sure not to approach or touch research objects.
- To see sea otters: from Elkhorn slough drive towards Moss Landing State Beach. Park where the 1 freeway crosses the Elkhorn Slough Channel to see sea otters playing in the Slough Channel.

TOP 5 HITS

1. Walk the South Marsh Loop Trail (2.2 miles).
2. Take a guided kayak tour.
3. Walk out to Hummingbird Island (about 0.3mi).
4. Walk the Five Fingers Trail (1.12 mile loop), to Parsons Overlook Extension to see shorebirds, seals, otters, and mud flats.
5. 5. Watch sea otters play in the Elkhorn Slough Channel.

Teeming with life!

SHOW NOTES

Elkhorn Slough is a National Estuarine Research Reserve that is teeming with interesting plants and wildlife. Slough is another word for swamp, which describes the views you'll see when visiting. But there is much more here, including the important estuary. Estuaries, including the surrounding wetlands and swamps, are where rivers meet the sea. This allows the mixing of fresh water from inland and saltwater from the sea, called brackish water, which creates one of the most productive ecosystems in the world. There are unique plant and animal communities that have adapted to brackish water.

Many visitors choose to explore this area by kayak, providing great views of the habitats and animals like sea otters, harbor seals, and over 300 types of birds! Exploring the bridges and walkways will also provide great wildlife viewing opportunities. The rich waters' edge of mud and soil is a productive area where seabirds probe for insects and crustaceans. During the nesting and migration seasons, these mud flats are critical as birds require more high-nutrient foods, where they may find and eat midge-larvae and earthworms.

NORTH
US
101

VIDEOS AND RESOURCES

MY PLAYLIST

music, books, podcasts...

SUGGESTED JAM

Track: I Remember California

Artist: R.E.M

MEET THE LOCALS

get to know the flora, fauna and features

OWL BOXES

Owl boxes provide homes for owls in areas where rodent control is needed. Farmers and others will hang owl boxes so owls will stay nearby, be safe and hunt on their property. Owls are nocturnal and hunt mice, rats, gophers and other small rodents.

COAST LIVE OAK

Coast live oaks grow acorns which are an important food for deer and birds. Woodpeckers love to build their homes in these oaks and peck holes all over the trunk and branches to store acorns in for food. Its leaves are between 1-2 inches long which is smaller than other oak trees.

PICKLEWEED

The pickleweed got its name because its stems look pickle-like and it also tastes salty. It can survive in extreme salty conditions that most other plants die from. Any salt that the plant absorbs is stored in its pickle like ends causing them to turn reddish and fall off.

LONG-BILLED CURLEW

The long billed curlew digs into the damp earth to find crabs, shrimp and earthworms with its long curved bill. It can be found in wetlands, beaches, and areas with low water. Its nest is called a scrape because they scrape a shallow hole into the ground and line it with leaves and twigs.

ACORN WOODPECKER

This bird stores its nuts in tree holes they make called granaries. A granary tree can have up to 50,000 holes in it. They pack the nut in so tight that even squirrels can pry them out.

MY REVIEW

Write about your experience

TOP 5 HITS

1. Observe the giant pacific octopus, see how it moves and find its beak.
2. Watch the video presentations in the auditorium.
3. Watch the sea otter feeding.
4. Touch the rays and tide pool creatures.
5. Find your favorite jellyfish and see everything!

PRO TIPS

Season: Fall and winter, between 2-6 p.m. for less crowds, Open All Year Long

Difficulty: Easy, ADA accessible

Time Needed: Day trip

- Take the time to do Free online classes and educational programs offered on the Monterey Bay Aquarium website.
- Ask the front counter for animal feeding times and trainer programs. They are not on the map or information paper they give you as you walk in.
- Take your time, don't rush yourself or your kids. There is a lot to see and observe in each tank.
- Take a nature journal and sketch your favorite sea animals.
- Watch the otter video presentation before the otter feeding time. It will teach you about what you will see in the otter tank.
- They have food at the aquarium for lunch or you can get a re-entry stamp at the front door and leave to get food.
- The Aquarium Parking Structure is a 10 min walk from the aquarium. 4-5 blocks.
- Reaching the tentacles exhibit is tricky. To reach the tentacles exhibit you need to go up the escalator by the auditorium, then take a left and go down the corner stairs.

Under the sea

SHOW NOTES

The Monterey Bay Aquarium is more than just an aquarium with beautiful exhibits. In addition to inspiring all who visit to become stewards for ocean conservation they also work to rebuild sea otter populations, to transform fisheries, and bring awareness and change in plastic pollution. They also have a seafood watch team that is working to make seafood more sustainable.

Fall in love as you see ocean creatures up close. Watch playful otters, vibrant jellyfish, and sneaky octopuses as they swim, feed and interact with each other in their life size tank environments. Gently touch tide pool creatures such as sea stars and urchins in the touch tanks and feel the slimy texture of a ray swimming by. The ocean is an incredible place full of life and wonder, fall in love all over again on your next visit.

VIDEOS AND RESOURCES

MY PLAYLIST

music, books, podcasts...

SUGGESTED JAM

Track: Monterey

Artist: Eric Burdon & The Animals

MEET THE LOCALS

get to know the flora, fauna and features

SEA OTTER

The sea otter has the densest fur of any mammal with about 1 million hairs per square inch! Humans only have about 100,000 hairs on their entire head. They're the only marine mammals to use rocks as tools to break open shells.

SEA LEMON NUDIBRANCH

Nudibranchs are a shell-less mollusk and part of the sea slug family. They sense food using feathery antennae and have feathery gills on their backs for breathing. Their bright colors come from the foods that they eat. Predators spit them out because they smell and taste bad.

GIANT PACIFIC OCTOPUS

The giant pacific octopus is known for its bulging eyes, rounded head and eight legs. It can use its tentacles to build a den around itself by moving rocks into place. They are also very good at camouflage which they can use to communicate with other octopuses.

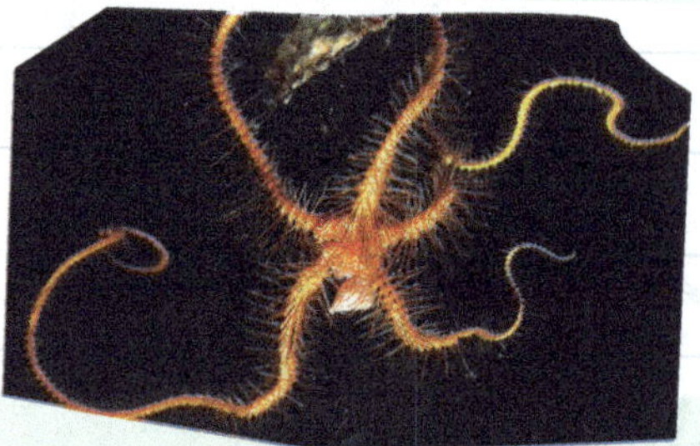

BRITTLE STAR

Brittle stars are the fastest moving echinoderm. It is in the class Ophiuroidea meaning "snake-like" which describes how its five arms move. Brittle stars are more fragile than starfish and their arms can break off easily if they are picked up by humans or to get away from prey.

CALIFORNIA MORAY

The California moray is a long, snakelike fish that has to open and close its mouth to breath. This is because it doesn't have gill covers to push water over its gills. A morey has 2 jaws, one in its mouth and one at the back of its throat that springs forward and drags its prey into its throat.

MY REVIEW ☆☆☆☆☆

Write about your experience

17

BIG SUR

CENTRAL COAST

DATE ____________________

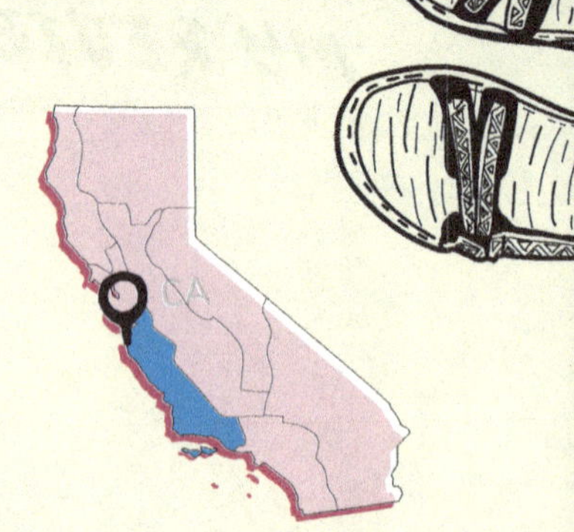

TOP 5 HITS

1. Hike Soberanes trail and see redwoods, 2.5 miles round trip.
2. Check out the purple sand and Keyhole Rock at Pfeiffer Beach, .9 mile round trip.
3. Hike to Partington Cove Trail, 1 mile round trip.
4. Walk the McWay falls trail to see a tidal fall, .5 mile round trip.
5. Take pictures at Bixby Bridge.

PRO TIPS

Season: April- June when the waterfalls are the biggest (but the park is the busiest) Sept.-Oct. when temperature is at its best and before the winter rainy season.

Difficulty: Easy hiking and lots of scenic driving

Time Needed: 1-2 Days

- There is no cell service in Big Sur
- There are also no street signs that tell you where the hiking trails and beaches are.
- Get or print a paper map and mark where you want to go before you go to Big Sur. Print out all your directions to each location. Include the miles of how far each stop is from each other. (ex: Partington Cove Trailhead is 6 miles south of Nepenthe Restaurant.)
- The purple sand at Pfeiffer Beach are deposits of manganese garnet that have washed down from the surrounding hills.
- The trail down to Partington Cove is easy to miss. Type in the GPS coordinates 36.1770, -121.6937 and mark it on a map. Park on the side of the road next to the trail. The trail is on a curve on the road and looks like a cattle gate.
- Soberanes Trail- there is a bluff access trail across the street from the parking with a small waterfall, The main trail goes inland and will take you to redwoods and lush landscapes that are different from the coastal areas. It's a great area to picnic and relax.
- Stay till sunset and watch the clouds roll in beneath you from any pull off on the side of the road.
- Bring binoculars and a good camera for a better view of McWay Falls. You can only see it from the overlook. No beach access.

SHOW NOTES

It's true that the word big is representative of this 90-mile stretch of coastline- from its big peaks, rivers and gorges, to big trees and far-spreading wildfires. These 800 acres are home to coastal redwoods, chaparral, coyotes, mountain lions, foxes, deer, and many more animals. The clear waters of the 15.7-mile-long Big Sur River influence the ecosystems throughout the park.

Check out McWay Falls, one of just two tidal falls in all of California. During high tide, this 80-foot-tall waterfall empties directly into the Pacific Ocean. Don't miss the amazing purple sand at Pfeiffer Beach, the cascading tidal fall at McWay Falls! The sand washes down over the cliffs above, transporting eroding manganese garnet that is particularly prominent after a rainfall. This water-laden landscape makes it possible for unique plants to grow here, and one big example is the California Redwood. They grow well in coastal habitats, where daily fog provides sufficient moisture in the summer months and frequent rains allow hydration in the winter months. The near-coast environment influences the critical cycle of creating clouds, fog, and precipitation.

Big Syr!

MY PLAYLIST

music, books, podcasts...

VIDEOS AND RESOURCES

SUGGESTED JAM

Track: Big Sur

Artist: Jack Johnson

MEET THE LOCALS

get to know the flora, fauna and features

MCWAY TIDAL FALLS

A tidal fall is a waterfall that empties directly into the ocean. Mcway Falls used to always flow directly into the ocean, but a landslide created the sandy cove at the base of the falls in 1983. This 80 foot waterfall flows year round and now only flows directly into the ocean at high tide.

BIXBY CREEK BRIDGE

The Bixby Creek Bridge is the tallest single span arch bridge in the world. It is considered the gateway to Big Sur and one of the most popular Instagram spots on the west coast. There are lookout spots on the bridge, but the bridge is only 24 feet wide so it is not safe to walk on it.

PURPLE SAND

The purple sand at Pfeiffer Beach is made by the erosion of manganese garnet that washes down from the hills when it rains. The best time to see lots of the purple garnet sand is after a rainy day, near the creek. The brownish sand on the beach is mostly broken down quartz.

PFEIFFER KEYHOLE ARCH

Pfeiffer Keyhole Arch is the second most photographed place in Big Sur. People say it looks like a door to a new world, especially in the winter near the winter solstice when you can see the sunset through the arch. Do not go into the arch or swim, there are sneaker waves and strong currents.

CALIFORNIA CONDOR

In 1982, the worldwide California condor population was at 23 total condors! We now have over 400 wild birds in the wild. These massive birds have a wingspan over 9 feet! They are scavengers and love to eat large animal carcasses called carrion.

MY REVIEW

Write about your experience

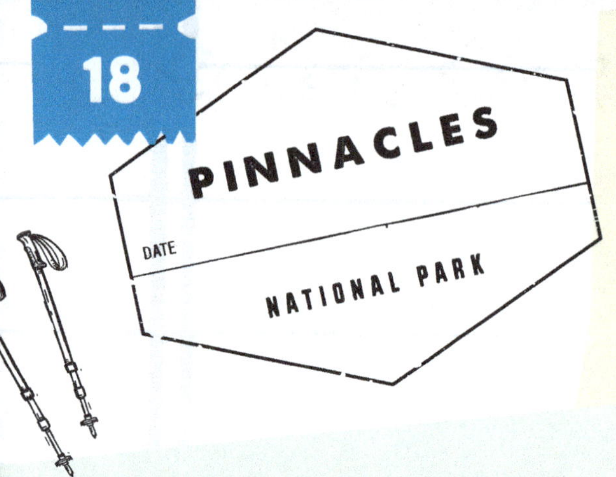

PRO TIPS

Season: Spring, fall and winter, less crowds and best weather. Summer and early fall get triple digits.

Difficulty: Easy-moderate

Time Needed: 2 days

- No cell service in the park.
- There are two different entrances, the East Entrance and West Entrance that will take you to different parts of the park.
- There is not a road that takes you through the park from one side to the other. You have to drive 1 hr. 15 min. around the park to reach both sides.
- Do one side of the park per day, You can hike to the other side but I don't recommend it. You can get lost on the windy crisscrossing trails or stuck on the other side of the park and need to hitchhike back to your car.
- Take flashlights to see in the talus caves. The caves are only open around the last week of Mar., most of Oct., and sometimes partly open Nov.- Feb.
- Hike with lots of water there is none along the trails, water refill is only in the parking lots.
- East Side of Park, park at Bear Gulch to start your day hikes, if the parking is full you will have to hike 2.2 miles from the Visitor Center to reach the trailheads.
- Go early to get good parking, parking lots can fill up as early as 8 a.m.

TOP 5 HITS

1. Moses Spring Trail to Bear Gulch Cave Trail to reservoir, 2.2 mile loop.
2. Explore Bear Gulch Talus Cave.
3. Rest and sketch at Bear Gulch Reservoir.
4. Hike Balconies Cliffs- Cave Loop through the Balconies Talus Cave, 2.4 mile loop.
5. Walk along the Jawbone Trail from the West Visitor Contact Station to get a view of the spires.

This Place Rocks

SHOW NOTES

Historians and biologists have called this National Park the land "born of fire" - because an erupting volcano was the major event that formed the famous Pinnacles found here. When two tectonic plates collided and rearranged millions of years ago, it eventually caused multiple volcanic eruptions that continued to deposit layers of volcanic rock. Over time, this volcanic field shifted, sunk, and eroded – creating high, pointed rocks called pinnacles that continued to be shaped by wind and precipitation.

Steep, narrow canyons became filled with jumbled masses of boulders, varying in size, that tumbled down from the cliffs above. These talus caves are unlike many other caves formed out of limestone found elsewhere in the country. One of the talus caves here, called Bear Gulch, is home to one of the largest known maternity colonies of Townsend's big-eared bats. Compared to the rest of the region, Pinnacles National Park hosts a great diversity of reptiles, including eight lizards, fourteen snakes, and one turtle – the Southern Western Pond turtle.

VIDEOS AND RESOURCES

MY PLAYLIST

music, books, podcasts...

SUGGESTED JAM

Track: Highway 101

Artist: Social Distortion

MEET THE LOCALS

get to know the flora, fauna and features

CALIFORNIA CONDOR

In 1982, the worldwide California condor population was at 23 total condors! In 2003 Pinnacles began working to protect and repopulate the condor population. We now have over 400 wild birds in the wild. These massive birds have a wingspan over 9 feet!

TALUS CAVE

Talus caves look like narrow chasms filled with boulders. The Balconies caves and the Bear Gulch caves are two areas of talus cave to explore in Pinnacles National Park. Falling rocks and the forces of weathering continue to change the physical construction of the caves.

HOLLY LEAF CHERRY

Holly leaf cherry is a small evergreen that is part of the rose family. Small white flowers bloom in the springtime. As an adult tree or shrub, it supports a variety of moths and butterflies, and produces cherries that are eaten by many birds and mammals.

SPIRE

A spire is a smooth column of rock that tapers from the ground upward. Forces of weathering and erosion wear away the rock to create these stacked towers. These impressive rock structures are protected here and are what gives Pinnacle National Park its name.

CHAMISE

Chamise is the most widely distributed chaparral species in California's shrubland communities. Its white flowers grow in clusters. The dense shrubland created by chamise provides cover for amphibians and reptiles, and nesting birds.

MY REVIEW ☆☆☆☆☆

Write about your experience

19

PIEDRAS BLANCAS ROOKERY

DATE

SAN SIMEON

PRO TIPS

Season: Best times to visit; Jan.-Feb. birthing and breeding season, April-May molting season

Difficulty: Easy, ADA accessible boardwalk

Time Needed: 1-3 hours

- To get to the rookery type in "Elephant Seal Vista Point San Simeon" into your GPS.
- Stop and use the restrooms at William Randolph Hearst Memorial Beach before you go see the elephant seals. These are the nearest restrooms to the seal viewing area.
- Elephant seals can be seen here almost year round but are most abundant on the beach during the winter mating/ birthing season and the spring molting season.
- Bring snacks and jackets, it can get windy. Be prepared to stay a while to watch the seals.
- Talk to the volunteer docents at the viewing area, they are knowledgeable and can tell you all about what you will be seeing, they will point out new babies, bulls and answer all your questions.
- Hearst Castle is located 5.2 miles south of the rookery at Elephant Seal Vista Point.
- There is a smaller parking lot .5 mile north of the rookery where the Piedras Blancas Light Station trail starts. 3.2 mile round trip hike, or you can hike 4 miles round trip from the rookery parking.
- Check online for days, times and price of the Piedras Blancas Light Station tours. https://www.piedrasblancas.org

TOP 5 HITS

1. Walk the south boardwalk and check out the elephant seals.
2. Watch the elephant seals interact with each other, especially the bulls.
3. Picnic at William Randolph Hearst Memorial Beach.
4. Walk down to the beach at William Randolph Hearst Memorial Beach and relax.
5. Hike to Piedras Blancas Light Station, 3.2 mile round trip hike, and take a docent led tour.

Front row seats!

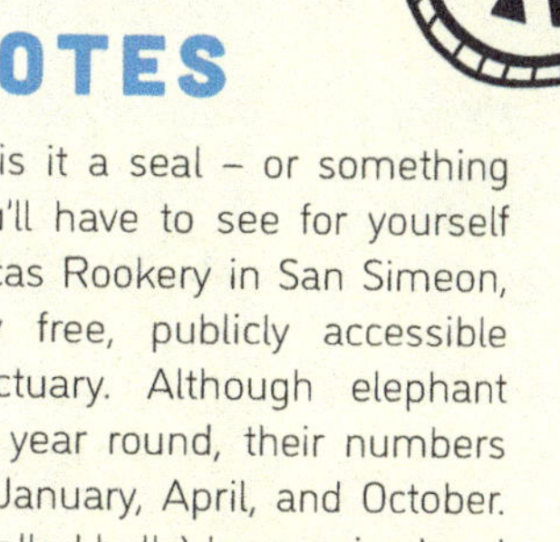

SHOW NOTES

Is it an elephant – is it a seal – or something totally different? You'll have to see for yourself at the Piedras Blancas Rookery in San Simeon, California: the only free, publicly accessible elephant seal sanctuary. Although elephant seals visit this area year round, their numbers are greatest during January, April, and October. By January, males (called bulls) have arrived and are fighting for mating rights amongst each other. Females soon arrive and the breeding season continues into the late winter months, when the adults return to sea.

These marine mammals are true seals. Bulls may reach enormous sizes, measuring 16 feet in length and weighing 5,000 pounds. Elephant seals were hunted nearly to extinction for their oil-rich blubber, which was used for lamp oil and lubrication. By 1900, the northern elephant seal was presumed extinct and the United States soon granted them protection. Males again began appearing on California's coast in 1965, and the first pup born since protections were enacted was documented here in 1975.

VIDEOS AND RESOURCES

MY PLAYLIST

music, books, podcasts...

SUGGESTED JAM

Track: San Simeon

Artist: Goldfinger

MEET THE LOCALS

get to know the flora, fauna and features

ELEPHANT SEAL PUP

A pup is born with a black coat and is 3-4 feet long and weighs about 70 lbs. The mother seal will nurse it for about a month, before she will return to the sea. The pup is then left alone fasting for 8-10 weeks on the beach while it learns to find its own food and swim.

ELEPHANT SEAL ADULT FEMALE

An adult female can weigh between 900- 1800 lbs. She arrives at the beach in the winter to give birth. She will stay to nurse her pup for a month then mate with the "Alpha Bull" a few times before returning to the sea. A group of female seals is called a harem.

ELEPHANT SEAL JUVENILE MALE

Juvenile male seals are between 2-5 years old. Around 7 years old it will grow a large inflatable nose "proboscis" that will overhang its lower lip by 8 inches. They come to shore once a year to shed their shin or 'molt'. These young males will play-fight to prepare for battles as adults.

ELEPHANT SEAL BULL MALE

A bull elephant seal has a large proboscis that looks like a small elephant trunk. During breeding season Bulls will make loud calls with their proboscis and fight to claim the beach and breed with all the female seals. A bull will fast for about 3 months to keep his claim on the female seals.

COYOTE BRUSH

Coyote brush plants produce either male or female flowers. Its leaves are covered with a thin wax that prevents transpiration, water loss from leaves. Its leaves were also used by Native Americans to reduce swelling. Its wood was used to make houses and arrows.

MY REVIEW ☆☆☆☆☆

Write about your experience

20

MONTAÑA DE ORO

DATE

STATE PARK

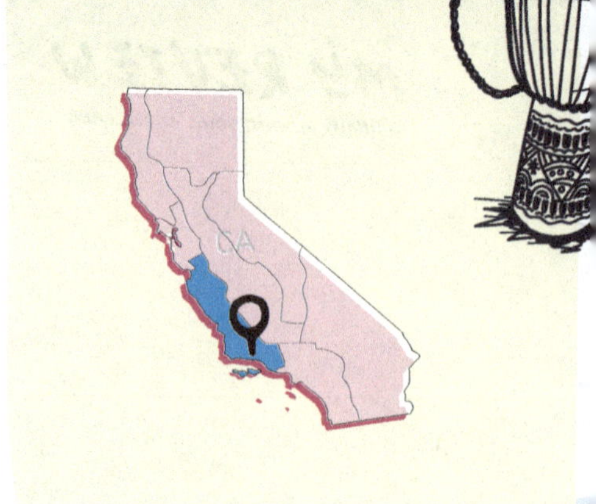

TOP 5 HITS

1. Hike to Hazard Reef and explore the tidepools, .9 mile round trip.
2. Hike the Bluffs Trail along the cliffs to see crazy rugged cliffs, 1-4 miles or as long as you want to walk.
3. Walk the path through the Native Plant Garden (Holloway Garden) by the Spooner Ranch House.
4. Relax and picnic at the beach at Spooners Cove.
5. Explore more tidepools at Corallina Cove.

PRO TIPS

Season: Good year round, best time to visit is in the spring when plants are blooming and at low tide.

Difficulty: Easy

Time Needed: Day trip

- Check out all the overlooks on the Bluff Trail. The rock cliff outcroppings are unique with their ancient sea floor rock layers (Miguelito Shale) sticking out at different angles.
- Tread lightly at tidepools, only touch the animals as hard as you would touch your own eyeball.
- This state park has been preserved in its plant and wildlife habitats. Native plants flourish here and give this park its beauty. One plant that you will see that is not native is the Eucalyptus Tree from Australia which was planted for timber. Eucalyptus grows quickly but the need for timber was never high enough for it to be profitable, so it has been left to grow across the California Coast as an invasive species.
- The native garden is a must see. It is well maintained and has a large variety of full grown and unique native plants.
- Check out the Spooner Ranch House. It lets you see what life was like and it's still furnished like it was in the early 1900s.
- If you only have time for one tidepool area go to Hazard Reef, the tidepools here are the best in the area.
- You need to hike along the Bluff Trail to get to Corallina Cove.

SHOW NOTES

Peace and solitude, magnificent scenery, rugged cliffs, and pristine beaches can all be found inside Montaña de Oro State Park. The name translates to "Mountain of Gold," which is a reflection of the beautifully colored wildflowers that blanket the park each spring.

The area's soil and climate support an array of native plants. Morro manzanita chaparral occurs in two distinct dense stands within Montaña de Oro State Park, mixed with other native plants like chamise, wedge-leaved ceanothus, and coast live oak. These native plants stabilize soils and maintain natural communities over the long term. This also creates an environment for mushrooms, bryophytes, and lichens to grow, and provides cover for wildlife.

tide pool time!

VIDEOS AND RESOURCES

MY PLAYLIST

music, books, podcasts...

SUGGESTED JAM

Track: California

Artist: Joni Mitchell

MEET THE LOCALS

get to know the flora, fauna and features

FUCHSIA FLOWERED GOOSEBERRY

The fuchsia flowered gooseberry has bright red flowers that hang downwards beneath its leaves. If you look at the flower with a magnifier you will see balls of moisture on the hairs of the flowers. Be careful when you get close to the plant because it has sharp long spines all over its stems.

SOAP PLANT

The soap plant grows from bulbs underground. Pieces of these bulbs were used by Native Americans as soap. They also used it to stun fish, because it has a chemical that paralyzes their gills. Moths pollinate the strong smelling, fragrant soap plant flowers at night.

LINED SHORE CRAB

The lined shore crab can spend up to 70 hours on land before it needs to go back underwater. It hides under rocks and in cracks on rocky shores and tidepools. It will eat mussels, snails, flies, seaweed, decaying organisms and even each other.

GOOSENECK BARNACLE

Gooseneck barnacles have a long fleshy stem that looks like a neck and live attached to rocks and flotsam. Above their stems they grow many plates around their body for protection. When it is underwater it uses its feathery feet that they use to filter feed and breath.

CALIFORNIA BUCKWHEAT

Buckwheat seeds can be eaten as cereal, ground into flour, or as a substitute for rice. The buckwheat flowers are rich in nectar that attract bees to the plant. These flowers dry up and turn reddish brown and brittle as the plant dies. New plants will grow from the fallen seeds.

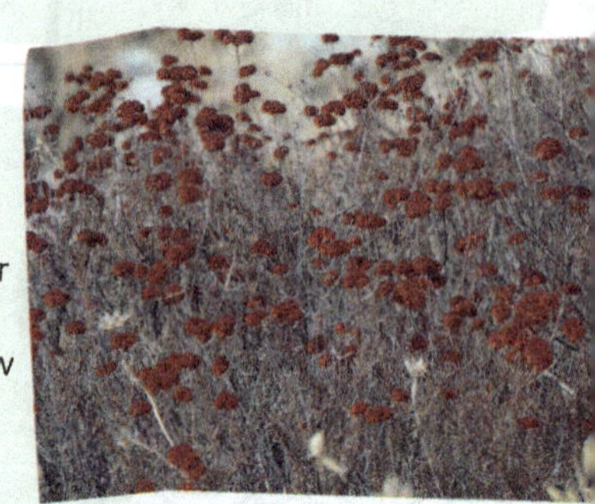

MY REVIEW ☆☆☆☆☆

Write about your experience

21

LIZARDS MOUTH ROCK

LOS PADRES NATIONAL FOREST

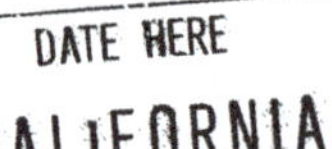

CALIFORNIA

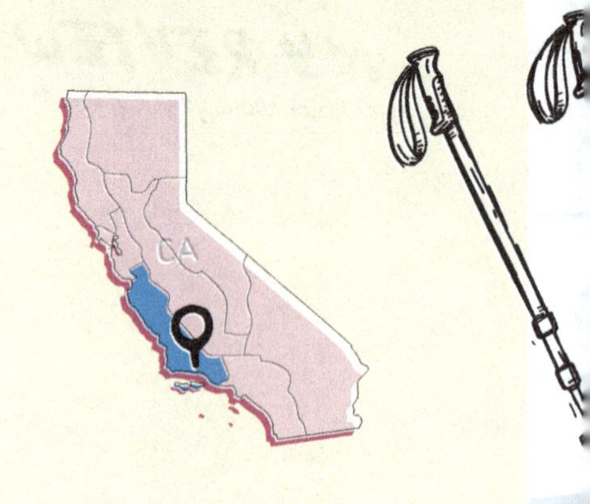

PRO TIPS

Season: Year round

Difficulty: Easy short trail and rock scrambling

Time Needed: 1-2 Hours

- The trailhead is located about 100 yards before the Winchester Canyon Gun Club. Park on the side of the road before the Gun Club. The trailhead is on the same side of the street as the Gun Club.
- The trailhead sign is hidden behind a tree, look for a large metal water drain pipe on the side of the road with a trail next to it.
- If you're there around sunset you can watch the marine layer or low clouds roll onto the land from the sea.
- From the top of the Lizards Mouth Rock formation, when you are facing away from the ocean, there is a small trail to the right that leads under the formation.
- Bring a light jacket, this area can get really windy.
- This is a great area to wander, rock scramble and explore.

TOP 5 HITS

1. Hike to Lizards Mouth Rock .3 mile round trip.
2. Take pictures from the top of Lizards Mouth Rock.
3. Find and explore the small caves and cracks in the rocks.
4. Take in the view of Santa Barbara and the Channel Islands.
5. Find tafoni inside caves and inside Lizards Mouth Rock.

SHOW NOTES

Several hiking trail avenues lead to this area of massive sandstone outcroppings, including the most famous: Lizards Mouth Rock, which really does look like a lizard's head with its mouth open. Some visitors think it looks more like a frog. The sandstone has been carved over time by wind and water that helped create the large pocket forming the reptile's "mouth." Water can also work over time to shape sandstone, forming caves, tafoni, and crevices. Sandstone is formed when deposits of sand are cemented together by smaller particles like those the size of silt or clay, which may be delivered via rivers, waves, or wind.

The trail to Lizards Mouth Rock is short but rocky, so sturdy hiking shoes are a must. From this vantage point, visitors can experience unparalleled views into Santa Barbara, Goleta and the Channel Islands. The area is a favorite for bouldering and rock climbing. The Santa Ynez Mountain Range was created by movements of the Santa Ynez Fault during the Cenozoic age. Most of the rocks here are sandstones and shales, with some limestone in certain places.

Big Mouth

MY PLAYLIST

music, books, podcasts...

VIDEOS AND RESOURCES

SUGGESTED JAM

Track: Santa Barbara

Artist: Rebelution

MEET THE LOCALS

get to know the flora, fauna and features

TAFONI

Tafoni are small honeycomb-like formations in sandstone. Slightly salty rainwater seeps into the rock and dissolves sand and cement particles. As the water dries some of the particles condense and harden forming the honeycomb like walls, loose particles are blown or washed away.

WIND CAVES

The wind caves in the sandstone at Lizard Mouth Rock are shaped mainly by water. Water will dissolve the cement between the quartz grains in the sandstone then wind and water will carry the cement grains away. This process continues forming caves in the sandstone!

SANTA CRUZ ISLAND

Santa Cruz Island is the largest of the 8 Channel Islands. It is home to species of plants and animals that live nowhere else on earth like the island fox and island scrub jay. The island also has many sea caves including one of the largest sea caves in the world, Painted Cave.

OUR LORD'S CANDLE

This plant was a major food source for native people. The roots and stalks could be boiled for food. Seeds and blossoms could also be ground, and eaten. The thorny stems could be used as sewing needles and the green leaves could be used to weave baskets and sandals.

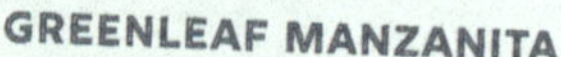

GREENLEAF MANZANITA

Manzanita is Spanish for little apple and was named after its small red berries that resemble little apples. A manzanita can be a small tree or large shrub. Its seeds will fall to the ground and remain dormant for years till a fire comes and cracks them open.

MY REVIEW ☆☆☆☆☆

Write about your experience

PRO TIPS

Season: Spring-fall

Difficulty: Easy

Time Needed: Day trip or 2-3 days backpacking style camping

- These Pro Tips and Top 5 Hits are specific for Santa Cruz Island, Scorpion Anchorage.
- If you are new to ocean kayaking book the adventure sea cave tour with Santa Barbara Adventure Company
- If you are an experienced ocean kayaker you can bring your own kayak and you need to reserve a kayak spot on the ferry to take it to the island.
- Can rent kayaks for ages 5+ at Channel Islands Kayak Center on the mainland before you go and you need to reserve a kayak spot on the ferry to take it to the island. The Kayak Center will take the kayaks to the ferry dock for you. You will need to check in and then put them on the ferry yourself.
- There is no kayak rental on the island.
- You can rent snorkeling gear on the island.

TOP FIVE HITS

1. Kayak around sea caves and kelp of Scorpion Anchorage.
2. Hike Cavern Point Loop Trail, 2 miles loop.
3. Look for and watch the curious island foxes.
4. Snorkel around the kelp forest in Scorpion Cove.
5. Look for dolphins and whales on the ferry ride.

- There is NO food to buy on the island, bring all your food and water. There is a water spigot at the campground.
- Ravens and foxes can open zippers. Make sure to protect your food. Fox boxes are available near restrooms to put your food if needed.
- There are restrooms near the dock on the island.
- When you hike the trails near the cliffs stay away from cliff edges. These are actively eroding cliffs and can break.

SHOW NOTES

You've probably explored a forest many times – but have you ever experienced an underwater forest? An amazing kelp forest exists beneath the crystal waters of Channel Islands National Park! Kelp grows in tall, stretchy strands. Gas-filled bubbles help buoy the plant upwards towards the surface of the sea, allowing it to absorb sunlight - drawing energy deep into the ocean and powering the beginning of a food chain. In this underwater world, keystone species play an important role in maintaining the balance of the entire ecosystem.

Diving, kayaking, and snorkeling are popular activities here that allow visitors to get up close and personal with the unique features of life on isolated islands. There are also numerous trails to traverse on land, ranging from the easy walking trails within Scorpion Valley to the rugged pathways in the Montañon area. The island houses tall peaks, one of the world's largest sea caves, and an amazing 60 endemic plant and animal species! The island fox is considered a keystone species on the islands because of its complex connection with the land's other species.

Cavern Point

VIDEOS AND RESOURCES

MY PLAYLIST

music. books. podcasts...

SUGGESTED JAM

Track: Channel Islands

Artist: The Bronx

MEET THE LOCALS

get to know the flora, fauna and features

SANTA CRUZ ISLAND
CHANNEL ISLANDS
NATIONAL PARK

SANTA CRUZ ISLAND LIVE FOREVER

Santa Cruz Island live-forever is an endemic, federally threatened succulent plant species that grows only on rocky patches of Santa Cruz Island. It has just a few visible leaves during the winter, and blooms clusters of white star-shaped flowers.

ISLAND FOX

The island fox is one of the smallest foxes on earth and is a descendant of the common gray fox. Without any predators in the Channel Islands, they hunt during the day heavily relying on an excellent sense of smell. Keep a close eye on your food, these small foxes can open your bags.

OYSTERCATCHERS

The black oystercatcher nests on islands and uses its heavy bill to pry or smash shells open. When the shell is partly open it will cut the adductor muscle that holds the shell closed, then eats. They hunt on rocky shores and tidepools eating mostly mussels, limpets and shellfish.

GARIBALDI

Adult garibaldi fish are bright orange and fiercely territorial. Garibaldi are a protected species and are named California's state marine fish. Their habitat is the cooler waters of kelp forests, which provide protection from predators, food sources, and places to reproduce.

GIANT KELP

Giant kelp is a type of marine algae that often grows in dense patches. The plants provide habitat for over 1,000 marine plants and animals. Nine types of kelp grow in the Channel Islands, but giant kelp is the largest and most dominant species.

MY REVIEW ☆☆☆☆☆

Write about your experience

SIERRA NEVADAS

This place is home to three incredible National Parks (Yosemite, Sequoia, Kings Canyon), the highest mountain peak in the lower 48 (Mount Whitney), the largest tree on the planet (Sequoia), the oldest trees on the planet (Bristlecone Pine) one of the tallest waterfalls in the country (Yosemite Falls), the largest alpine lake in North America (Lake Tahoe)... and a ton of incredible wildlife. On this tour you can hear a Moaning Cavern followed by a float through the natural pools and cavern of Natural Bridges in Calaveras County. Want to see a place that looks like you've landed on another planter? Then head to Mono Lake to see the amazing Tufa Towers. If you'd rather see a towering series of columnar-jointed basalt and swim at the feet of Rainbow Falls, then check out Devils Postpile National Monument. At Mammoth Lakes and Mountains you can find world-class ski slopes and great mountain biking among other things. Lets not forget the rock climbing mecca of Yosemite where you'll find Half Dome and El Capitan. Cap it all off in a relaxing soak in the natural hot springs of Grover Hot Springs State Park. You really could spend a lifetime in the Sierras and never get bored.

23

LAKE TAHOE

SIERRA NEVADAS, CA

DATE ______________________

PRO TIPS

Season: Spring, fall for less crowds

Difficulty: Easy

Time Needed: Day trip

- This information is for the South Lake Tahoe area.
- Go to D.L. Bliss State Park (Lester Beach) early in the day. Parking near the beach is limited and fills up early. Bring paddle boards or kayaks to better enjoy the beach and reach the rocks to cliff jump.
- Kayak or paddle early in the day before the wind picks up.
- Eagle Falls can be seen from both sides of the main road. The main trail starts next to the parking lot. There is also a short path on the other side of the main road where you can see Fannette Island and a view of Emerald Bay.
- Park along Venice Dr E. Road at Truckee Marsh and look for trails along the road to enter the water. You can paddle through the marsh all the way to Lake Tahoe. Watch for turtles, birds, frogs and other creatures. There is also a walking path at the end of the road that will take you to the beach.
- If you want to kayak or paddle Emerald Bay you will need to rent a kayak at Emerald Bay. The trail is 2 miles round trip and steep so you can't carry kayaks down to the beach.

TOP 5 HITS

1. Visit Emerald Bay State Park, 2 miles round trip.
2. Hike to Eagle Falls, .5 mile round trip.
3. Enjoy Tahoe's beaches such as Lester Beach and jump off rocks.
4. Walk the Balancing Rock Nature Trail, .5 mile round trip.
5. Kayak Truckee Marsh.

kayak the jewel of the sierra

SHOW NOTES

The largest alpine lake in North America, Tahoe reaches a maximum depth of 1,645 feet. That's a depth that could fit the whole Eiffel Tower one and a half times and still have space remaining. It's all thanks to an ancient volcano, Mount Pluto. Lava from an eruption millions of years ago created a dam, which transformed what was once a valley basin into an enclosed area. This new area was then filled gradually by rain and melted snow from the surrounding Sierra Nevada Mountains.

The first thing many visitors notice about the lake is its dazzlingly blue, crystal clear coloration. While most lakes host large amounts of algae, which produce a cloudy, green color, Tahoe's high elevation has historically prevented algae growth. Additionally, the rocks, soils, and wetlands surrounding the lake filter the water that feeds into the lake, stopping sediments that would make Tahoe murky.

VIDEOS AND RESOURCES

MY PLAYLIST

music, books, podcasts...

SUGGESTED JAM

Track: Lake Tahoe

Artist: David Beck

MEET THE LOCALS

get to know the flora, fauna and features

FANNETTE ISLAND

There's only one island on Lake Tahoe, and that's Fannette Island. Keep your eye out for a tiny castle structure on top of the island, which was built as a personal tea house around the same time as Vikingsholm Castle.

EAGLE FALLS

A set of carved, stone steps on the Eagle Falls Trail will lead you to these waterfalls while also giving you a great view of the surrounding forests. If you care to continue on, you'll also be treated to a beautiful lake.

VIKINGSHOLM CASTLE

Inspired by churches and fortresses, Vikingsholm Castle might make you feel like you've stepped into historic Scandinavia. In order to be as authentic as possible, some sections of the building don't even use nails, pegs, or spikes, choosing medieval European techniques instead.

BELTED KINGFISHER

You can identify a belted kingfisher through their blue-gray coloration and distinct, V-shaped stripe across their chests. Kingfisher beaks look a bit like daggers, and there's a reason for that--these birds hunt by diving into the water and spearing tiny fish with them.

WETLANDS

These combinations of land and water are what make the clear waters of Lake Tahoe possible. They are also home to many fish, birds and other wildlife. Conservationists are working to restore areas like the Upper Truckee River Marsh to help keep the Tahoe waters clean and clear.

MY REVIEW ☆☆☆☆☆

Write about your experience

PRO TIPS

Season: Spring -fall (late summer can have sudden afternoon thunderstorms)

Difficulty: Easy

Time Needed: Day trip

- The boardwalk/ transition trail merges with the Burnside Lake Trail to the waterfall, and gives you views of the meadow. (Take the boardwalk to the trail)
- If you have paid for pool admission, day use parking is included.
- Dogs are allowed on a 6ft leash for hiking, they are not allowed at the hot springs pools
- You must get online and reserve a 90-minute time slot, and pay the hot springs entrance fee. If a thunderstorm shows up and they see lightning in the distance, the pool will close for 30 min.
- There are two trailheads to get to the waterfall. The shortest trail starts at the hot springs pool parking lot called the hot springs cutoff trail, the main trail starts at the overflow parking lot at the north end of Quaking Aspen Campground.
- Bathrooms are located in the campground and near the entrance.
- Bring all your meals and snacks into the park with you. Nearby Markleeville is small and has limited dining, which may close early or is only open on the weekends.
- Do not leave windows cracked when food is in your car, bears can rip cracked windows open to get your food.

TOP 5 HITS

1. Swim and soak at the hot springs.
2. Burnside Lake Trail, 3 mile round trip hike to the waterfall along Hot Springs Creek. (11 mile hike to the lake)
3. Rock scramble on the rocks near the falls.
4. Walk through the ADA accessible boardwalk, Transition Trail, to see the meadow.
5. Cool off, play and take a dip in the creek on the North Creek or South Creek overlook trails by the campground bridge.

natural springs

SHOW NOTES

No matter how cold the weather is outside, Grover Hot Springs always maintains a toasty temperature of over 100 degrees Fahrenheit. It isn't humans keeping the springs warm--it's magma. That's because this area rests on a fault line. Fault lines are cracks in the earth's surface, and this one is caused because the plate that makes up the North American continent is constantly colliding with the Pacific plate. These collisions cause pressure, which forces the heavier Pacific plate underneath the American plate (a process called subduction), turning it into magma. The cracks in the Earth formed by this process are called faults.

Grover Hot Springs is heated by one of these faults, using a process called convection. In the late 1800s, settlers shaped the pools, combining hot and cold springs to reach an enjoyable temperature.

VIDEOS AND RESOURCES

MY PLAYLIST

music, books, podcasts...

CALIFORNIA 89

SUGGESTED JAM

Track: California

Artist: Bob Dylan

GROVER HOT SPRINGS

MEET THE LOCALS

get to know the flora, fauna and features

JEFFREY PINE

The tall Jeffrey pine tree is named after the botanist that first documented it. It has needle-like leaves in clusters of three and produces large cones that start out dark purple in color. Snap a needle or smell between the bark's crevices to discover this tree's interesting scents!

BIG SAGEBRUSH

The big sagebrush's gray-green leaves are velvety to the touch, and emit a powerful, clean smell. Despite its name, the big sagebrush is not actually a species of sage. Instead, it belongs to the same family as the sunflower.

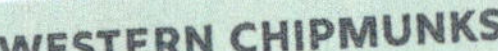

WESTERN CHIPMUNKS

Western chipmunks are small members of the squirrel family and have a varied diet. They most often snack on seeds, buds, fruits, and nuts, but will opportunistically eat fungi, insects, worms, and bird eggs. Expandable cheek pockets allow them to carry food to a cache.

HORSETAIL

Horsetail can grow in very wet soils and can reach five-feet tall. It has segmented green stems similar in appearance to bamboo and reproduces via spores. This non-flowering plant often grows into dense colonies.

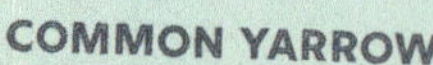

COMMON YARROW

Common yarrow has a high tolerance for drought. The plant grows up to three feet tall, has dark green lace-like delicate leaves, and clusters of flowers at the very tops of its stems from April to July. Flowers may be primarily white or pink.

MY REVIEW

Write about your experience

PRO TIPS

Season: Mar.-Sept.

Difficulty: Easy

Time Needed: Day trip

- Swim holes on Stanislaus River are located about 100 feet after the River Picnic Area by the bridge. There is parking on both sides of the bridge, the sign will say River Access Parking.
- There are three different stairways that take you down to the Stanislaus River swimming areas. This is a deeper river, bring life jackets.
- Bring life jackets for kids if you are thinking of jumping off of rocks near the bridge. The river flows faster near the rocks.
- A second swim area is located at Beaver Creek Picnic area that is shallower for smaller kids.
- The North Grove provides trail guides at the trailhead. Read it aloud as you walk around the grove. They look wordy, but are really well done and help you to understand the history of the forest and what you are seeing.
- Encourage kids to ask questions to the park rangers.
- Visit the Visitor Center before you hike the North Grove. It will teach you about the sequoias and other trees in the area. As you hike try and identify the different trees.

TOP 5 HITS

1. Hike the North Grove Trail, 1.7 mile loop.
2. Walk across a giant fallen sequoia.
3. Picnic, slow down and use your senses. Smell the trees and air. Listen for birds and sounds of the forest. Feel the bark of the different trees.
4. Jump in or play in the Stanislaus River.
5. Explore, hike and climb along the rocks of the Stanislaus River.

SHOW NOTES

Sequoias are more than just big trees--by volume, they're the most enormous living thing on Earth, with adaptations that allow them to grow up to 325 feet tall and live for up to 3,000 years. These plants reproduce through seeds found in small, green cones at the top of the tree. In order to open and drop these seeds, the cones need the help of something that would kill most trees: fire. Wildfires dry out a sequoia's cones, cracking them open and allowing them to drop their seeds hundreds of feet to the forest floor.

American Indians respected these groves for hundreds of years, but the Europeans that discovered them in the 1800s did not share this respect. They cut down the largest tree in the park, the "Discovery Tree", and used its stump as a dance floor. The second largest tree, the "Mother of the Forest", was skinned, allowing it to die from burns. You can choose to be kind and considerate towards nature by picking up trash and staying on trails at this park.

walk among giants

VIDEOS AND RESOURCES

MY PLAYLIST

music, books, podcasts...

SUGGESTED JAM

Track: California

Artist: The Hooks

MEET THE LOCALS

get to know the flora, fauna and features

CALAVERAS BIG TREES

GIANT SEQUOIA

Giant sequoias are the most massive trees on Earth and can live to be 3,000 years old. You can identify sequoias not only by their size, but also by their reddish-brown bark. These huge trees have huge appetites--just one adult sequoia can drink up to 800 gallons of water in one day!

PACIFIC DOGWOOD

Indigenous people used Pacific dogwood trees in many ways, including making brown dyes, curing stomach ailments, and weaving baskets. Look for oval leaves with pointed tips to find these trees, as well as bright red coloration in fall and large, white flowers in spring.

CALAVERAS MOTHER OF THE FOREST

The remains of this dead tree are famous within Big Trees State Park. The Mother of the Forest stood alive as a 321-foot-tall sequoia tree over 2,500 years old! Some of its bark measured two feet thick. Now it stands as a tall, burnt, bark-less stump.

SEQUOIA CONE

Giant sequoia trees start producing cones around ten years of age. Sequoia cones are about the size of a chicken egg, composed of even smaller seeds. There are both male and female cones, but only the female cones produce seeds that can grow new sequoias.

CALAVERAS FATHER OF THE FOREST

An extremely old giant sequoia tree lays fallen across the woodland floor in the North Grove at Calaveras Big Trees State Park, called the Father of the Forest. When it stood alive, it was believed to reach 450-feet tall and 112-feet around at its widest point.

MY REVIEW

Write about your experience

DATE

MOANING CAVERNS
ADVENTURE PARK

PRO TIPS

Season: Spring, summer, fall

Difficulty: Moderate, 235 spiral stairway, 1 mile downhill hike with 1 mile uphill back.

Time Needed: Day trip

- If you or your kids are claustrophobic or really scared of heights, Moaning Caverns might be scary or not for you. It is a deep, one large chamber cavern that starts by having you walk down a narrow stairway and then you walk down a 235 stair spiral staircase to the bottom.
- Most of your cave formations can be seen from the back side of the spiral stairway closest to the wall. Go down and up at the end of the group so you can take your time and see them.
- Bring a river tube to float through Natural Bridges Cavern, the water is cold and chest deep. Inflate it at your vehicle and carry it down. Bring a backpack to carry it back up deflated.
- Floating through the cavern is a must, most of the cavern is not visible through the entrance.
- Celebrate your trip by eating foods related to formations you saw in caves. (Bacon, chocolate, popcorn, grapes, cauliflower, soda"straws")

TOP 5 HITS

1. Take the Spiral Tour of Moaning Caverns.
2. Look for cave formations.
3. Pan for minerals or fossils at Moaning Caverns Adventure Park.
4. Hike to Natural Bridges Cavern then float through it, 2 mile round trip.
5. Catch and release crawdads down river from Natural Bridges Cavern.

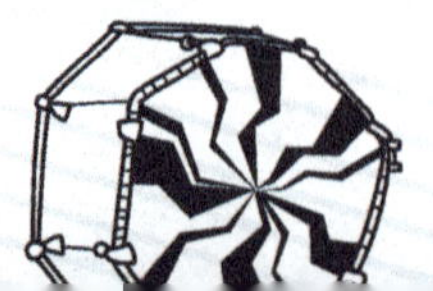

go underground

SHOW NOTES

While many Central California destinations allow you to see the power of geology from above ground, Moaning Caverns takes you below the surface into the eerie and beautiful world of caves. Plunging down a staggering 165 feet, this is the largest public cave chamber in California. In other words, if you tipped it on its side, Moaning Caverns could fit a line of three and a half semi trucks.

Bones found at the cave floor suggest that ancient people fell through holes on the surface and met their demise inside. Some of these bones date at least 12,000 years (around the time that mammoths went extinct in North America). More recently, tourists at Moaning Caverns in the mid-1800s saw the caves by candlelight as they were lowered down in buckets. Your visit will be much more safe--you'll have the chance to climb down a historic spiral staircase constructed with steel from a World War One battleship.

VIDEOS AND RESOURCES

MY PLAYLIST

music, books, podcasts...

SUGGESTED JAM

Track: California

Artist: Dr. Dog

MEET THE LOCALS

get to know the flora, fauna and features

STALACTITES

These icicles shaped structures hanging from cave ceilings, are created when water containing dissolved minerals drips from the top of the cave, leaving tiny bits of these minerals behind. You can remember what a stalactite looks like by remembering that it holds tight to the cave ceiling.

STALAGMITES

Though stalagmites appear to be growing up from the ground, they actually are the result of water dripping from the ceiling. This water leaves small amounts of minerals where it drops, which build up slowly after thousands of years to produce a stalagmite.

CAVE BACON

Cave bacon is a type of flowstone that looks just like a piece of delicious breakfast food. The layered appearance of cave bacon shows times in geological history where the flow of the water making the formation changed--perhaps there was less rain, or a change in the minerals in the water.

SODA STRAWS

Just like the straws you might use at a restaurant, soda straw cave formations are stalactites developed in the shape of hollow tubes. As cave water drips through these tubes, it leaves a tiny rim of deposited mineral at the bottom of the soda straw, helping it grow longer.

POPCORN

Cave popcorn, also known as cave grapes, is formed as water seeps through the roof of the cave and forms small drops of water. These drops either splash to the ground leaving minerals behind or evaporate leaving the minerals in the shape of small balls.

MY REVIEW ☆☆☆☆☆

Write about your experience

27

DATE

YOSEMITE

NATIONAL PARK

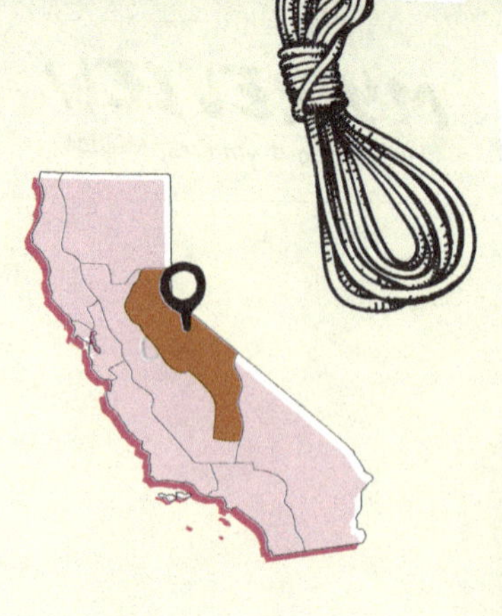

PRO TIPS

Season: Spring- fall, waterfalls are their biggest in the spring

Difficulty: Easy

Time Needed: 2-3 days

- A good place to see Glacial Striations is at Tuolumne Meadows on the flat rocks by the river just off of the Soda Springs/Parsons Memorial Lodge Trail.
- Bring tubes to float down the slow moving Merced River in Yosemite Valley.
- For a short kid friendly float, get in the river at Swinging Bridge and exit at Sentinel Beach. Drop your family off at Swinging Bridge then drive to Sentinel Beach to pick up your family and tubes. It's a great spot to relax by the river.
- Bring a bike to avoid riding the crowded shuttle, bike paths run along the entire Yosemite Valley and are mostly flat and not on the road.
- Rocks near waterfalls are slippery, be careful and watch children.
- Tunnel View is an overlook that is an easy quick drive from Yosemite Valley. It offers a fantastic view of the valley.
- A good place in Yosemite to see giant sequoias near Yosemite Valley is Tuolumne Grove, 2.5 miles round trip.
- The Merced Grove is near the West entrance but has a steep trail down to the sequoias and you have to walk along a dirt road as well. It is not a good trail for kids.

TOP 5 HITS

1. Admire the beauty of Yosemite Falls from afar and up close, 1 mile loop.
2. Bike or walk through the Yosemite Valley via Cook's Meadow boardwalk loop, 1 mile.
3. Rock scramble at Bridalveil Falls, .5 mile round trip.
4. Relax, swim, or float down in the Merced River at Sentinel Beach.
5. Hike to the top of Vernal falls, 2.4 miles round trip, or stop at the bottom, view the falls, and go back.

- Hike Halfdome (if your family ages and abilities allow) 16.5 miles round trip. Reserve a permit ahead of time. Permit lottery sign up is in March. A daily lottery is also available 2 days before your trip.

SHOW NOTES

The breathtaking shapes of iconic Yosemite features like Half Dome and El Capitan were made possible by powerful glaciers over two million years ago. The valley's story begins even earlier--100 million years earlier. Yosemite's granite was formed when magma hardened underground. This granite was much harder than the other rocks around it, and when those other rocks were worn away, the granite was left standing.

Throughout the creation of the Sierra Nevada mountain range, new rivers and volcanic activity took turns leaving gashes on the landscape and cutting canyons in the granite. This brings us to the importance of glaciers--about three million years ago, the Sierra Nevadas had become very tall and very cold. Though they've long since melted away, enormous masses of ice once dominated the landscape. In this lesson, you'll learn about the awesome power glaciers can have, and about how they shaped this distinct and breathtaking valley.

view of the valley

VIDEOS AND RESOURCES

MY PLAYLIST

music. books. podcasts...

SUGGESTED JAM

Track: Something that you Know

Artist: Jamestown Revival

MEET THE LOCALS

get to know the flora, fauna and features

HALF DOME

Half Dome was originally named "Tis-sa-ack" An Ahwahneechee phrase for Cleft Rock. It looks like a giant rock on top of a mountain that has been cut in half. It is formed from some of the hardest granite in the USA. There is a strenuous hiking route with cables that people like to take to the top.

MULE DEER

The mule deer's name comes from its huge, mule-like ears. These mammals are fast, sprinting up to 45 miles per hour. This comes in handy when sharing habitats with hungry mountain lions. Look for mule deer in the mornings and evenings, as they are most active during these times.

ROCK CLIMBER ON EL CAPITAN

Yosemite is a rock climber's paradise, and one of the most famous climbing spots is El Capitan. Known locally as "El Cap", this rock formation is about 3,000 feet tall. Miwok tribal legend has it that the first creature to scale this wall was an inchworm!

MEADOW

A meadow is an open habitat or field filled with grasses, herbs and other non woody plants. The meadows of Yosemite are lush, thick with plant life and support plants that use shallow surface water. They act like sponges absorbing the water that melts from the peaks above.

BLACK BEAR

Don't let the name fool you; black bears can also be brown or even blond. These are the smallest bears in North America, but they are still dangerous. If you see one, give it lots of space. Raise your arms to look bigger, make noise by talking to it and slowly move away.

MY REVIEW

Write about your experience

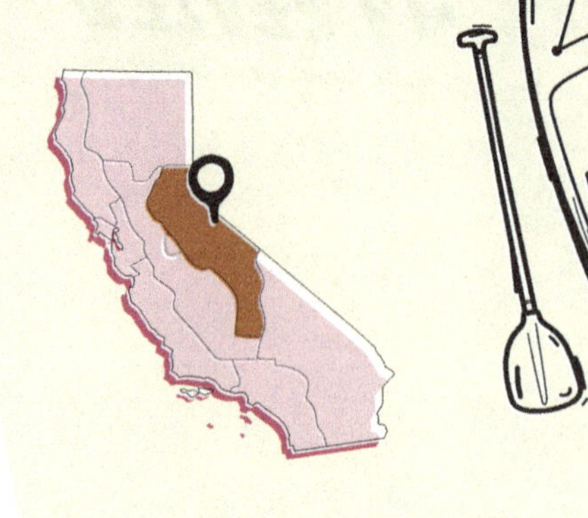

PRO TIPS

Season: Mar.-Oct.

Difficulty: Easy

Time Needed: Half Day

- The water is 2.5 times more salty than the ocean. It's too salty for fish to live here but if you look closely in the water there are a lot of brine shrimp.
- You can get in the water and swim or float at South Tufa.
- Bring extra fresh water to rinse yourselves off afterwards if you plan to swim. The salt left on your skin will look scaly and can be uncomfortable.
- Don't drink the water or put it in your mouth. It's really salty and will make kids cry.
- Bring your own paddle boards and kayaks. Local companies do kayak tours only. No rentals.
- Don't go within 100 feet of the tufas on your kayaks and boards, this is to protect them and the osprey that nest there.
- There are several small trails to walk around the tufas, explore and find hidden coves and beaches.

TOP 5 HITS

1. Walk the boardwalk ADA trail to the tufas at South Tufa Area, .8 mile round trip or loop walk.
2. Float or swim in the lake.
3. Kayak or paddleboard around the tufa towers.
4. Look for osprey nests on the tufas and brine shrimp in the water.
5. Hike the Panum Crater 2.1 mile loop on the crater rim, or .2 mile hike to the rim.

- There is a small brown street sign on the 120 (Mono Lake Basin Rd.) that says Panum Crater at the road to Panum Crater. (The sign is low to the ground and as high as the surrounding sage brush, so drive slowly to see the sign, it will be a dirt road.) The dirt road is fairly straight so if you are going on a windy road you are on the wrong road.
- Don't collect obsidian or pumice on the Pumice Crater hike. It's everywhere along the crater, let's keep it this way for future visitors.
- The Mono Basin Visitor Center is located just north of Lee Vining.

SHOW NOTES

These mysterious, crumbling pillars of white rock are called tufa towers. Mono Lake is full of carbonates (substances a bit like baking powder), and underwater springs carry calcium from below ground up into the lake. Carbonates and calcium produce a chemical reaction when combined, creating limestone. Over time, the limestone created at the spring openings built up higher and higher, eventually forming a tufa tower that is up to 30 feet tall.

Water can enter Mono Lake, but there is no way for it to leave. Through many millennium, evaporation caused these salts and minerals to build up inside Mono Lake, making the water here 2.5 times as salty as the ocean. The hardy species that call this place home, though, don't mind. Alkali flies, for example, spend most of their lives underwater. Brine shrimp also thrive here and provide food for millions of migratory birds.

Tufa! Tufa! Tufa!

VIDEOS AND RESOURCES

MY PLAYLIST

music, books, podcasts...

SUGGESTED JAM

Track: Mono

Artist: Zero 7 featuring The Hidden

MEET THE LOCALS

get to know the flora, fauna and features

TUFA

Tufa is a white, crumbly rock created by underwater chemical reactions. If you visited Mono Lake 100 years ago, you wouldn't have been able to see any iconic tufa towers. That's because the tufa you see now was only revealed when the lake was partially drained in 1941.

OSPREY NEST

Look to the tops of tufa towers and you might spy osprey nests. These fish-eating birds add more to their nests each year, allowing them to grow to up to ten feet tall! In the spring and summer, the nests you see may also house a clutch of eggs or fuzzy chicks.

ALKALI FLIES

The tiny insects that cover Mono Lake's shoreline are no average flies. They grow specialized hairs that trap a layer of air and allow them to breathe in water! On a day with calm water, you might be able to see alkali flies walking underwater along the lakebed. (They won't bite you.)

BRINE SHRIMP

These miniature shrimp, about the length of a fingernail, live in the trillions in Mono Lake. Brine shrimp have white coloration and 22 arm-like appendages, which are so small they look like hairs. For millions of migrating birds, brine shrimp make a perfect on-the-go snack.

BIG SAGEBRUSH

The big sagebrush's gray-green leaves are velvety to the touch, and emit a powerful, clean smell. Despite its name, the big sagebrush is not actually a species of sage. Instead, it belongs to the same family as the sunflower.

MY REVIEW

Write about your experience

29

TOP 5 HITS

1. Admire Devils Postpile, .4 mile one way (check out the formation from above and below)
2. Hike to Rainbow Falls from Devils Postpile, 2 miles to the falls.
3. Swim in the pool and river at the base of rainbow falls. Hike 1.3 miles back to shuttle stop #9 afterwards.
4. Walk the Sotcher Lake Nature Trail, 1.2 miles trail going around the left side of the lake. The full loop takes you up a tall hill. Just walk the part by the lake.
5. Swim or play in the water at Sotcher Lake to cool off after all your hiking.

PRO TIPS

Season: Only open from about July- mid Oct. (changes every year according to snowfall) https://www.nps.gov/depo/planyourvisit/basicinfo.htm check for yearly park opening date

Difficulty: Easy-moderate

Time Needed: Day trip

- You must get shuttle tickets to get to Devils Postpile from July to mid Sept. It is possible to drive to Devils Postpile mid Sept.-mid Oct. (park closing)
- You can bring dogs on a leash as long as they wear a muzzle on the shuttle.
- Pack plenty of snacks, a swimming suit, and a picnic lunch to take with you. Your shuttle ticket expires when you return to the Mammoth parking lot or lodge area.
- There is a snack shop at shuttle stop #9 if you need more food, bathrooms, and a water refill spicket to refill water bottles. Shuttle stop #8 also has a water refill area and a ranger station with maps and junior ranger booklets.
- There are 2 ways to reach Rainbow Falls, 1) hike the 2 mile trail starting at the Devils Postpile Formation, or 2) hike 1.3 miles from Shuttle stop #9
- Sotcher Lake has small sand areas that give you access for swimming in the lake. There is pumice (volcanic rock) along the trail, pick some up and throw it in the lake. See what happens...(it floats!)

SHOW NOTES

The story of Devils Postpile began between 80,000 and 100,000 years ago, in an age where Earth was home to animals such as neanderthals and giant sloths. This particular site was also home to lava--lots and lots of it. The lava that spewed from the Sierra Nevadas was particularly hot, with high iron and magnesium content (basaltic lava), which made it thin and runny. A river of it flowed down the Reds Meadow Valley, destroying everything in its path--everything, that is, except for a natural dam (likely made from rock left behind by an ancient glacier). When this lava river reached the natural dam, it pooled into an enormous lava lake. In some areas, this lake was 400 feet deep! Eventually, the lava cooled. When lava cools, it contracts, or shrinks. This shrinking caused the newly formed rock to crack into the beautifully shaped columns we can see today.

ancient rocks

VIDEOS AND RESOURCES

MY PLAYLIST

music. books. podcasts...

SUGGESTED JAM

Track: Something that you Know

Artist: Jamestown Revival

MEET THE LOCALS

get to know the flora, fauna and features

MULE DEER

Mule deer are mostly brown with a black-tipped tail and have large ears. Males of this species grow new antlers each spring, shedding the previous year's antler growth in February after the breeding season. Adult mule deer can reach over 200 pounds, browsing on shrubs, trees, and forbs.

JEFFREY PINE

The tall Jeffrey pine tree is named after the botanist that first documented it. It has needle-like leaves in clusters of three and produces large cones that start out dark purple in color. Snap a needle or smell between the bark's crevices to discover this tree's interesting scents!

LODGEPOLE CHIPMUNK

The lodgepole chipmunk is found only in California and Nevada. They are named for their preference to live among pine and fir forests (particularly Lodgepole pine). The females of this species are larger than the males. They make many vocalizations to communicate with each other.

SIERRA GOOSEBERRY

Sierra gooseberry is a short (under four-feet) shrub that produces red to purple berries that are covered in skinny spines. Some animals eat the fruit, like black bears and rodents, and several eat the leaves – including mule deer and bighorn sheep.

COLUMNAR BASALT

Basalt is a type of rock formed from a volcano's lava. As the lava cooled, under certain conditions it cracked into regular hexagonal shapes, forming the Columnar Basalt you may see here. Although basalt is a very common rock, it's rare to observe these long, solid columns.

MY REVIEW ☆☆☆☆☆

Write about your experience

PRO TIPS

Season: Summer

Difficulty: Easy-moderate, mostly downhill bike path

Time Needed: Day trip

- There are free ranger led hikes to McLeod Lake. Check the Mammoth Lakes Visitor Center for times.
- Take the FREE trolley from Mammoth Lakes up to Horseshoe Lake, this trolley also takes bikes!
- Rent a bike or take your bike on the trolley up to Horseshoe Lake. The bike ride back to Mammoth Lakes is mostly downhill and spectacular. Small kids can do it.
- Bike rental places will not let you put their bikes in your truck, you will need to ride them to the shuttle.
- The Horseshoe Lake Loop is a beginner mountain bike trail. Great for kids.
- When you are biking down from Horseshoe Lake to Mammoth, stop and see the top of Twin Falls next to Lake Mamie then stop again next to the first twin lake and see the falls from the bottom.
- If you want to do even more mountain biking, Mammoth Mountain has a large mountain bike park for all skill levels. This is not free.
- There is no parking at the trolley. You will need to find parking then walk there or bike from the bike rental shops.
- Some parking is located at Lakes Bike Path Trailhead on the corner of Minaret Road and Lake Mary Road.

TOP 5 HITS

1. Ski, Snowboard, or tube at the resort in winter. Bike it in summer.
2. Bike or hike Horseshoe Lake Loop, 1.2 mile loop.
3. Drive to Convict Lake and hike the Loop Trail, 2.5 mile loop.
4. Stop at Twin Lakes to view Twin falls and have a picnic.
5. Bike from Horseshoe Lake back down to Mammoth Lakes Basin Trolley on the Lakes Basin Path. 5.2 miles.

SHOW NOTES

In the winter, skiers race down the snowy slopes of the local resort. Summer visitors explore the many miles of trails nearby on mountain bikes and by foot. Climbers tackle harrowing pitches on both rock and ice. Though the name may lead you to believe it is the home of prehistoric fossils, Mammoth Lakes was actually named after the Mammoth Mining Company, which drew the first European settlers here during the area's 1878 gold rush.

Overlooking all of Mammoth's activities is the beautiful Mammoth Mountain volcano, reminding us that everything in sight rests precariously close to active faults and craters. You can get a fantastic volcano view while hiking from Horseshoe Lake to McLeod Lake. This trail is short, but it presents lots of opportunities for learning and fun. It follows the McLeod Fault (a fracture in the earth's crust). Active faults, which are common in Central California, are faults in which the pieces of crust around them are still moving and causing geological activity.

Twin Falls and Twin Lakes

VIDEOS AND RESOURCES

MY PLAYLIST

music, books, podcasts...

SUGGESTED JAM

Track: Mammoth Lakes

Artist: Great Wolf Lodge

MEET THE LOCALS

get to know the flora, fauna and features

LODGEPOLE PINE

The lodgepole pine has a long, slender trunk. It can grow around 160 feet tall. Their 3 inch long cones can stay closed for years and will only open in the extreme heat of a forest fire. Its common name originates from when natives would utilize the straight trees to build teepees.

LICHEN

Lichens are actually two living things surviving as one! A single lichen is made up of a fungus plus either an alga or cyanobacterium. The fungus part of the lichen cannot produce its own energy, so it lives alongside another organism capable of producing energy from sunlight.

GOLDEN-MANTLED GROUND SQUIRREL

The small and agile golden-mantled ground squirrel prefers dense thickets with plenty of cover to hide in. It's often found within forests of coniferous trees, aspen, and manzanita, where it eats a wide omnivorous diet of vegetation, nuts, many insects, and even young birds or lizards.

CORN LILY

Corn lilies grow in moist mountain meadows and display green football-sized leaves when fully grown. In late summer, the plant produces a long shaft of cream-colored flowers. All of the plant is toxic if ingested, especially its roots.

TWIN LAKES WATERFALL

This water feature exists among the dense woodlands between Lake Mamie and Twin Lakes, within Mammoth Creek. The Twin Falls overlook has amazing views of the lakes and surrounding mountains. This waterfall, which is just east of Horseshoe Lake, tumbles about 250-feet.

MY REVIEW

Write about your experience

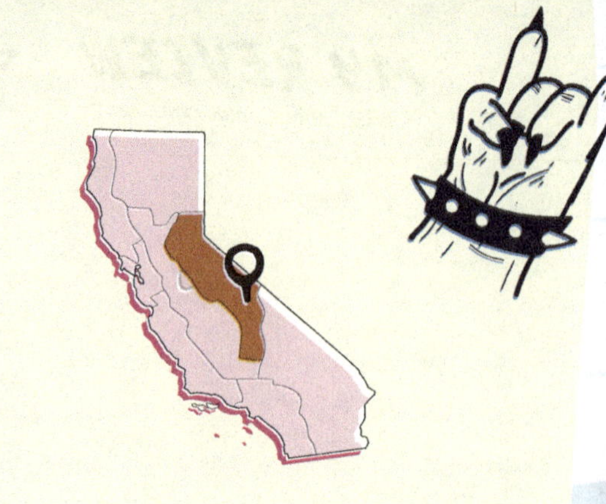

TOP 5 HITS

1. Visit the enormous General Grant Tree and walk through The Fallen Monarch. .3 mile loop trail.
2. Hike the Big Stump Trail to see the Mark Twain Stump, 2 miles round trip.
3. Observe the power of Roaring River Falls .5 mile easy walk round trip.
4. Picnic at Grizzly Falls and play in the stream and base of the waterfall.
5. Hike to Zumwalt Meadow .6 mile round trip.

PRO TIPS

Season: Spring, summer, and fall

Difficulty: Easy

Time Needed: 1-2 Days

- Mark Twain Stump and the Shattered Giant are both located in Big Stump Grove at the first parking lot near the park entrance. Do this trail first.
- Big Stump Grove was once heavily logged in the 1880s, it's a great place to see the big stumps and nature repairing the damage. It's also a good place to see sequoias that are not fenced in.
- The General Grant Tree is the busiest area of the park, many visitors come to see this then leave without seeing the rest of the park.
- There is a long 40 drive that separates the sequoia areas from the waterfalls. Because of the long drive this area isn't as busy. It has spectacular granite wall views similar to Yosemite NP.
- Grizzly Falls Picnic Area is a good place to get your feet wet and touch a waterfall.
- Don't go in the river at Roaring River Falls, people like to climb on the rocks to get a better view, but it's dangerous don't touch the water.
- There is also a cave at the bottom of the canyon. Book a 45 min tour of Boyden Cavern ahead of time. Closed in the winter.

SHOW NOTES

Army men in the mid 1800s called it the roughest land in the country. Naturalist John Muir declared it "a rival to Yosemite". Regardless of who you ask, Kings Canyon National Park is an awe-inspiring landscape, with powerful waterfalls, ancient sequoias, peaceful meadows, and dramatic valleys carved by glaciers.

Kings Canyon National Park, originally intended to protect a small area of sequoias from logging, was established in 1890 as General Grant National Park. Fifty years later, lots more land was added to the park and it was renamed Kings Canyon National Park after one of the area's most prominent valleys. Another of the park's most memorable features is its enormous redwood trees. A tree here dubbed General Grant is the second largest tree in the entire world (by trunk volume), with a height of 267 feet, a circumference of 107.6 feet, and a diameter of 40 feet (the largest diameter of any sequoia). This giant is young for a sequoia, at only about 1,650 years old.

peaceful vibes only

VIDEOS AND RESOURCES

MY PLAYLIST

music. books. podcasts...

SUGGESTED JAM

Track: Like a California King

Artist: Everclear

MEET THE LOCALS

get to know the flora, fauna and features

KINGS CANYON NATIONAL PARK

GENERAL GRANT TREE

The General Grant Tree is the second largest tree in the world by volume and is about 3000 years old. Its base is bigger than General Sherman, the biggest tree in the world. It was named after Ulysses S. Grant, and is also called "The Nation's Christmas Tree."

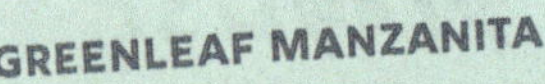

THE FALLEN MONARCH

The Fallen Monarch was hollowed out by wildfires so when it fell it was big enough for people to walk through. In the past this fallen tree has been used as a temporary home for loggers, a hotel, and stables for the US Cavalry.

GREENLEAF MANZANITA

Manzanita is Spanish for little apple and was named after its small red berries that resemble little apples. A manzanita can be a small tree or large shrub. Its seeds will fall to the ground and remain dormant for years till a fire comes and cracks them open.

MARK TWAIN STUMP

In 1891 this 1,350 yr. old giant sequoia was cut down so cross sections could be cut and sent to museums in London and New York. It took 2 men 13 days to cut it down. Go and observe its stump size and growth rings. It is now illegal to cut down a sequoia.

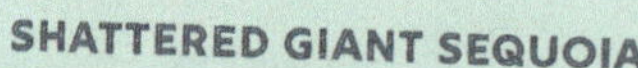

SHATTERED GIANT SEQUOIA

Sequoia wood is easily breakable. When loggers would cut down the sequoias they would have to lay down branches, called feather bedding, to soften the fall of the sequoia or it would shatter when it hit the ground. You can find a shattered giant on the trail in Big Stump Basin.

MY REVIEW

Write about your experience

TOP 5 HITS

1. Hike to General Sherman Tree, 1 mile round trip.
2. Hike Moro Rock, 400 rock steps that lead 300 feet in elevation to the top.
3. Big Trees Trail, 1 mile loop around sequoias and a marsh.
4. Climb on top of a fallen sequoia and hang on its strong roots.
5. Hike Tokopah Falls, 4 mile round trip trail.

PRO TIPS

Season: Spring, winter and fall

Difficulty: Easy-moderate

Time Needed: 2 days

- Hike Moro rock early or late in the day, the trail is in full sun. There are a lot of steps along a large dome to get to the top. There is a small rock wall along the trail edge but it can be a scary trail if you have a fear of heights.
- General Sherman is the busiest area of the park, expect a long line to take a picture in front of General Sherman, go at dusk for less crowds.
- To get to Tokopah Falls, park at the end of Lodgepole Campground near the bridge, walk across the bridge to find the trailhead.
- Don't swim in the Kaweah River by the Tokopah Falls Trail. People have drowned here, it has swift strong currents.
- Many people who visit sequoia only go to see General Sherman and the other big trees, make sure to do the other hikes because they are less crowded and still impressive.
- Your vehicle can only drive through tunnel log if it is shorter than 8 feet tall. There is a small road to drive around it if your vehicle is too big.

sky scrapers

SHOW NOTES

Sequoia National Park was among the first national parks ever created, designated as such in 1890. Visitors for thousands of years--for this was home to American Indian tribes long before modern European discovery--have stood in awe of the trees here, which are the world's largest by volume and the third oldest on the planet. General Sherman, a tree you'll see on your Sequoia National Park visit, is the largest of all sequoias. At 275 feet tall and over twelve million pounds, it is 2.5 times longer and over 35 times heavier than the largest blue whales!

There was a time in early park history when tunnels were cut into sequoias in order to attract more people into the park. Thankfully, times have changed. The goal in the park now is to allow nature to run its course with only minimal human interference.

VIDEOS AND RESOURCES

MY PLAYLIST

music. books. podcasts...

SUGGESTED JAM

Track: Meet Me in California

Artist: Plain White T's

MEET THE LOCALS

get to know the flora, fauna and features

GENERAL SHERMAN

The General Sherman tree is 275 feet tall and is over 36 feet in diameter at the base making it the largest tree in the world by volume. Its thickest branch is 6.8 feet thick! There is a fence around General Sherman to protect its roots from soil compaction from lots of visitors.

MORO ROCK

Moro Rock is a granite dome that rises 6,725 feet above sea level. It was formed from molten rock that formed 100 million years ago that rose upward and turned into granite as it cooled. You can hike the trail of a little over 350 stairs to the top of Moro Rock for an amazing view of sequoia.

SEQUOIA ROOTS

Search for a fallen sequoia to see its roots. A sequoia's roots grow shallow and wide; about three feet deep, and of the trees height wide! Because the roots are shallow they are able to quickly collect water from small amounts of rain and from melting snow.

FIRE BURN

After a fire a sequoia will heal itself by slowly covering its burn with new wood and bark. Sequoias need fire to survive. It releases seeds from their cones, creates ash nutrient rich soil, reduces competition from other trees.

DOUGLAS SQUIRREL

The Douglas squirrel (Chickaree) is an omnivore that eats seeds, fungi, insects, eggs, small animals, and even small snakes. It opens sequoia cones to eat their seeds. While eating, some of the seeds will fall to the ground, helping the sequoia to reproduce.

MY REVIEW ☆☆☆☆☆

Write about your experience

DESERTS

The desert makes up 38% of California. Technically, there are 3 different deserts in California: The Great Basin, the Mojave Desert and the Colorado Desert. Although they might appear as minimalist landscapes, deserts are surprisingly full of life and diversity. Over millions of years, extreme conditions have created some really cool adaptations in plants and animals that you can see first hand at the Living Desert Zoo and Gardens. Scramble the rocks at Joshua Tree National Park or spend a night stargazing in a place with no light pollution. Climb up and down the ladders of Painted Canyon of the Mecca Hills Wilderness or say hello to the hoodoos of Red Rock Canyon State Park. Maybe you want to escape the heat of the desert and explore San Jacinto Peak via the world's largest rotating tramway at Palm Springs Tramway. What does the lowest place in North America look like? Go to Death Valley National Park's Badwater Basin and see for yourself. Go bird watching at the Salton Sea where over 400 birds can be spotted. Hike The Slot, go cactus hunting....or if you're really lucky you just might see an explosion of color during a super bloom at Anza-Borrego Desert State Park. The desert can be inspiring and beautiful places to explore, photograph, meditate, hike, rock climb, and stargaze.

PRO TIPS

Season: Fall, winter, and spring when temperatures drop, spring may have wildflower blooms

Difficulty: Easy hiking, but be prepared for lots of driving as it's a large National Park

Time: 1-2 days

- No dogs are allowed on trails in the park, only at campgrounds and walking along backcountry roads.
- Stop at the Visitor Center and get a map of the park; cell service cuts in and out.
- Bring one extra gallon of water per person.
- Bathrooms are located at Badwater Basin, Artists Pallet, Salt Creek and Mesquite Sand Dunes.
- Bring sleds or boogie boards to slide down Mesquite Dunes.
- The drive to Ubehebe Crater is about 50 minutes from Mesquite Sand Dunes. Plan on the crater trip taking most of your day. You can still visit the dunes afterwards on the way back to the campgrounds.
- If you have time check out Devils Golf Course. It has unearthly looking rock salt deposits that make small ping sounds as some of the rock crystals burst apart as they expand in the heat. Stay quiet and listen carefully.
- The trail down to the bottom of Ubehebe Crater is steep and a lot of fun to go down, but it is very tiring to go back up. Take lots of water. It can be done with kids if you take a lot of breaks.
- When driving through Painted Canyon, make sure to stop at Artists Pallet to walk around and see the many colors of Painted Canyon up close. There is also a bathroom there for your convenience.

TOP 5 HITS

1. Walk and slide down Mesquite Sand Dunes.
2. Hike around Badwater Basin, 1.8 mile round trip (go to the end for the best view).
3. Walk the boardwalk at Salt Creek, 1 mile loop.
4. Drive through Painted Canyon.
5. Hike the rim of Ubehebe Crater, 1.5 mile loop, or take the trail to the crater bottom with a 600 ft. elevation drop.

desert adventures

SHOW NOTES

Death Valley is the largest National Park in the United States. It's home to salt flats, sand dunes, spectacular canyons, a volcanic crater, and much more! Death Valley is a desert, and it looks really dry when you look around, but it may surprise you. Water can be found at Saltwater Creek in the valley. Water is a powerful force of nature and has shaped the canyons, the many alluvial fans, and salt flats that are a highlight in Death Valley. The summer heat can reach up to 130 degrees Fahrenheit, which can evaporate your sweat and instantly leave you covered in your own salt. Visiting in the summer can be dangerous, but winter temperatures drop to the 60s and 70s, making it a great time to visit.

Death Valley became a National Monument in 1933, then expanded to become a National Park in 1994. In the early 1900s, it was home to silver miners who built several mining towns. Over time these mining towns have been washed away by flash floods, becoming ghost towns.

VIDEOS AND RESOURCES

MY PLAYLIST

SUGGESTED JAM

Track: Death Valley

Artist: LP

MEET THE LOCALS

get to know the flora, fauna and features

SAND DUNES

A sand dune can only exist if there is wind, eroding rock, and a place for sand to collect. Many insects and reptiles live on the dunes, burrowing into the sand to stay cool during the day. Keep an eye out for their tracks.

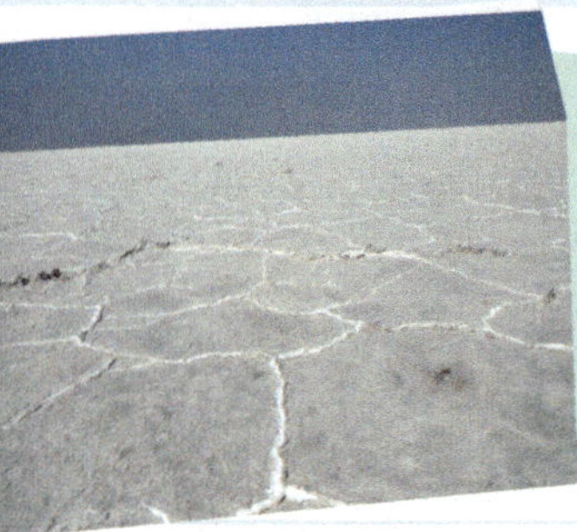

DESERT SALT FLATS

Desert salt flats are lakes that evaporate quickly after it rains. Salt and minerals are trapped in the dried lakebed, creating moon like surfaces. Badwater Basin Salt Flats is the lowest place in North America, at 282 feet below sea level.

ALLUVIAL FAN

Alluvial fans form when rain forms canyon rivers and flash floods that carry boulders, sand, and silt (called alluvium) out of the canyon and deposit them in the shape of a fan as the water disperses and slows. They have formed at the mouth of every canyon in Death Valley.

BEETLE TRACKS

Tracks from beetles, snakes, and other dune animals can be seen after a windstorm. The dunes record the tracks of every creature that walks on them like paint on a fresh canvas. The best place to find tracks are near the creosote bushes where the animals burrow and seek shelter.

PICKLEWEED

The pickleweed got its name because its stems look pickle-like and it also tastes salty. It can survive in extreme salty conditions that most other plants die from. Any salt that the plant absorbs is stored in its pickle-like ends causing them to turn reddish and fall off.

MY REVIEW ☆☆☆☆☆

Write about your experience

TOP 5 HITS

1. Hike the Hagan Canyon loop, 1.2 mile loop.
2. Find Turks Turban and look through Window Rock.
3. Hike Red Cliffs trail, 1 mile loop, explore hoodoos and rock scrambling.
4. Hike the 1.4 mile trail behind Ricardo's Campground and explore small caves and hoodoos.
5. Find rocks of all colors in the riverbed at the beginning of the Nightmare Gulch hike. Find but don't keep the rocks in state parks.

PRO TIPS

Season: Sept.-Jan. (some trails are closed for raptor breeding Feb. 1-July 1)

Difficulty: Easy, can drive to most of the rock formations.

Time needed: Day trip/ half day

- Hagan Canyon is famous for rock formations like Turk's Turban, Camel Rock, and Window Rock.
- Bathrooms are located at the Visitor Center and Red Rock Canyon.
- The road to Nightmare Gulch is a narrow dirt road; four-wheel drive is necessary.
- Wildlife is easiest to see near the Visitor Center due to water availability.
- There are fun rock formations for kids to climb at Ricardo Campground.
- Count the number of different colors of rocks you find at Red Rock Canyon.

hoodoos

SHOW NOTES

The colorful pink, red, white, and brown stacked cliffs of Red Rock Canyon offer visitors of all ages opportunities for rock scrambling and exploration. For thousands of years, Red Rock Canyon was used as a Native American trade route. Travelers could navigate through the canyon using distinct rock formations such as Camel Rock and Turk's Turban to guide the way.

The park has many diverse rock layers that are not only beautiful but offer opportunities to learn through paleontology, geology, and photography. Many of the rocks in the area have slowly been eroded by the wind and rain, forming tall stacked columns called hoodoos. The striking red rock layers have developed their color from the weathering of the iron and magnetite inside of them. These beautiful colors have drawn people to the area for thousands of years. Thanks to a natural process called oxidation, we will continue to see them for thousands more.

VIDEOS AND RESOURCES

MY PLAYLIST

music, books, podcasts...

SUGGESTED JAM

Track: When you get to California

Artist: Hoodoo Gurus

MEET THE LOCALS

get to know the flora, fauna and features

SILVER CHOLLA

The silver cholla is covered in dense clusters of spines that can easily be detached from the plant. It's spines are all different lengths and silver colored. When it blooms its flowers are a yellowish green. Do not touch, if you get it on your skin use tweezers or a comb for your clothes.

HOODOO

A hoodoo is a tall column of rock in the shape of a totem pole. It can have several layers of stacked sedimentary and volcanic rocks that give it unique colors. Wind and water slowly erode hoodoos until they fall down. These formations are typically found in hot, dry areas of the desert.

TURK'S TURBAN

Turks Turban was named by Rudolph Hagen, a German immigrant who acquired the land by purchasing mining claims. He let visitors come to see the park and its formations. A turban is a head covering made from winding up material. Turks Turban is a combination of hoodoos and red oxidized rock layers.

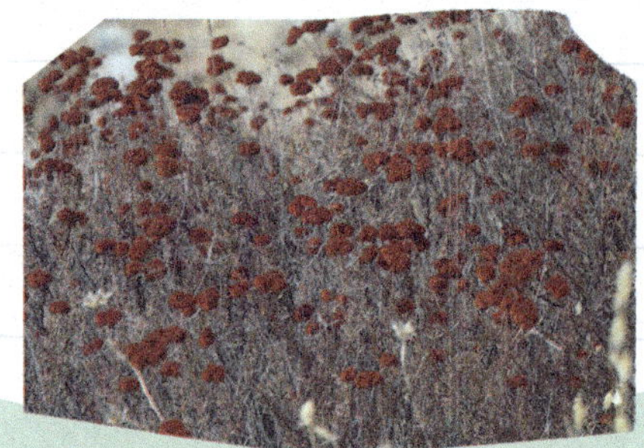

CALIFORNIA BUCKWHEAT

The California buckwheat can flower for months in the summer, even when the heat causes the other plants around it to stop blooming. In the winter the blooms dry up and become a coppery color and brittle. Its leaves and roots were used to treat headaches, mouthwash and even diarrhea.

BLACK-TAILED JACKRABBITS

Black-tailed jackrabbits are actually hares and not rabbits (which are larger than rabbits and born with fur). These speedsters can run up to 40 miles an hour and leap more than 10 feet! Their eyes are located high on the sides of their heads, allowing them to see almost 360 degrees.

MY REVIEW

Write about your experience

35

ANTELOPE VALLEY CALIFORNIA POPPY RESERVE

DATE HERE

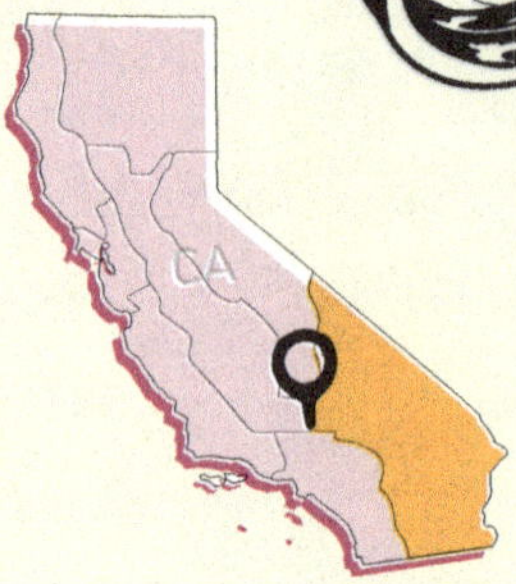

TOP 5 HITS

1. Stop and view a poppy field outside the reserve.
2. Hike .5 miles to Tehachapi Vista point for a good view of the blooms.
3. Claim a bench and sketch the different flowers. Observe and make notes.
4. Take lots of pictures.
5. Afterwards, visit the less windy Arthur B. Ripley Desert Woodland State Park, seven miles west, to make the most of your trip and entrance fee.

PRO TIPS

Season: Mid Feb.- May

Difficulty: Easy, walking trails with small rolling hills

Time Needed: Half day

- The reserve parking fee can be used for any other state park that day with the same or lower price.
- Drive carefully--cars stop suddenly to pull over to see fields of poppies and wildflowers on the way to the reserve.
- Don't pick the poppies or other flowers! It's illegal to pick them on state land.
- Don't go off the trails in the reserve; the flowers are fragile and are home to snakes and other animals.
- Go early in the morning to see the most flowers in full bloom and to beat the wind (which picks up as the day goes on).
- Bring a jacket. Strong winds can start suddenly.
- There is no shade, so bring lots of water and sunscreen.
- Parking fills up fast; go early in the day.
- Bring a sketchbook or nature journal and sketch the flowers of the reserve. Write about the different insects or wildlife you may see.

flower power

SHOW NOTES

The Antelope Valley California Poppy Reserve harbors the most consistent blooms of California's bright orange state flower, the California poppy, in the state. These bright orange poppies, which bloom from mid-February to mid-May, open during the day and close at night. They grow about 12-14 inches high forming rolling carpets of bright orange flowers across the reserve. Once they bloom, pollinators such as bees and beetles are necessary to pollinate these poppies so they can produce seeds for the next year's bloom.

The California poppy can be found in California, Mexico, and across the western United States. Its seeds are used by people across the world as a medicine for anxiety, pain, toothaches, and headaches. Poppy seeds have other uses as well. They are added to foods such as cakes, porridge and pastries. They can also be used to make soap, paint, and varnish.

Visiting the reserve, you have the opportunity to see the California poppy at its finest.

VIDEOS AND RESOURCES

MY PLAYLIST

music, books, podcasts...

SUGGESTED JAM

Track: California Poppies

Artist: Gina Royale

MEET THE LOCALS

get to know the flora, fauna and features

SILVER PUFF

Like a dandelion, the silver puff's seeds form a silvery puff that can be carried by the wind. Its flowers are yellow, and it has green, leaf-like phyllaries that extend beyond the blossoms, giving it a star shape.

CALIFORNIA POPPY

The California poppy is the state flower of California. It is a drought-tolerant plant that blooms from February to September. Its bright orange flower petals will open during the day then close up at night to avoid the cold and wind.

GRAPE SODA LUPINE

The grape soda lupine gets its name from its sweet smell that is similar to grape soda! Its bright purple flowers each have a yellow spot on them and grow spaced apart along long stems. Its leaves look gray but are really green and covered in silvery hairs.

BUMBLEBEE

The bumblebee is a large bee that is covered with many hairs for pollen to stick to. When it collects pollen, it can carry up to 75% of its body weight in pollen. Only the queen and worker bees can sting, but they are not aggressive. In the winter, bumblebees hibernate in the ground.

SYRPHID FLIES

Syrphid flies are also called hoverflies. They can often be seen hovering above a flower eating its nectar and pollinating the flower. They use mimicry to look dangerous like a black and yellow wasp, but are actually harmless to most animals. This mimicry protects them from predators like birds.

MY REVIEW ☆☆☆☆☆

Write about your experience

PRO TIPS

Season: Year round, hiking in the spring-fall, snow play in the winter

Difficulty: Easy

Time Needed: Day trip

- If you visit in the winter, wear a coat, a scarf, a beanie and gloves. (dress for the snow).
- The snow here can be icy; be careful not to slip.
- Bring a thick sled or boogie board for the snow.
- There is snow equipment rental, but it is not always open. Call ahead or bring your own.
- Check the weather report before going--call the Long Valley Ranger Station at (760) 327-0222 or check the bottom of the page at https://pstramway.com/
- In the summer, this is a great place to beat the heat of the valley below.
- Spring through Fall this is a fun place to hike around, explore, and take in the views.

TOP 5 HITS

1. Ride the Palm Springs Aerial Tramway.
2. Play in the snow.
3. Sled or tube down the hills.
4. Get hot chocolate at Mountain Station to warm up after snow play.
5. Take in the view of the valley below and of the giant gears that pull up the tram!

ride the tramway

SHOW NOTES

Mount San Jacinto State Park is the highest state park in California, at up to 10,804 feet above sea level! It was once used by native Cahuilla peoples, followed by European settlers, as seasonal hunting grounds for deer and gathering resources. In time, loggers came into the area, cutting down trees and introducing sheep and cattle that began to strip the meadows and hillsides. In 1897, the San Jacinto Forest Reserve was created by President Grover Cleveland to stop the logging and land destruction.

The aerial tram is one of the longest single-lift tramways in the world and carries visitors 2.5 miles up to Mountain Station in Mount San Jacinto State Park (at 8,516 feet in elevation).

Mount San Jacinto State Park is a unique place to escape the desert heat of the valley below. In the winter, when the Coachella Valley is still experiencing hot days, Mount San Jacinto has snow! There are only a few such places in Southern California. Spring through fall in the state park offers many miles of hiking.

VIDEOS AND RESOURCES

MY PLAYLIST

music. books. podcasts...

SUGGESTED JAM

Track: When you get to California.

Artist: Hoodoo Gurus

MEET THE LOCALS

get to know the flora, fauna and features

PALM SPRINGS TRAM

The Palm Springs Tramway is the world's largest rotating tram. This tram car will take you 2.5 miles up to Mount San Jacinto State Park at the top of the mountain. The tram slowly spins as it travels up, so every spot on the tram gives you a great view!

STELLER'S JAY

The Steller's jay is a forager. It finds seeds, nuts, eggs, and nestlings and buries them to store for food in the winter. It can hold several nuts in its throat as it searches for food. Watch out! Steller's jays steal food from humans as well as other birds. Don't give them food.

LODGEPOLE PINE

The lodgepole pine has a long, slender trunk. It can grow around 160 feet tall. Their 3 inch long cones can stay closed for years and will only open in the extreme heat of a forest fire. Its common name originates from when natives would utilize the straight trees to build teepees.

WHITEHEADED WOODPECKER

Whiteheaded woodpeckers love to eat large pine seeds, that's why they can be found in forests that have sugar pine and ponderosa pine trees. The female woodpeckers have a white head while the males have a patch of red on the top of their heads.

SUGAR PINE

The Sugar Pine is the biggest and tallest pine tree, growing up to 200 feet tall. Its cones can grow up to 20 inches long, that's almost 2 feet! Its wood is used for window and door frames, doors and piano keys. They can live longer than 500 years.

MY REVIEW

Write about your experience

TOP 5 HITS

1. Hike the Andreas Canyon Loop, 1.2 mile loop 200 ft. elevation gain.
2. Splash in the oasis, or sit on a large rock by the water and sketch.
3. Attend a free Ranger Talk or Interpretive Hike.
4. Look at the palm frond huts and grinding mortars at the bottom of the hill near the start of the Palm Canyon hike, .4 mile round trip.
5. Hike to the Seven Sisters Waterfall in Murray Canyon, 4.7 mile loop 450 ft. elevation gain. For a shorter hike take the same trail in and out, about 4 miles round trip.

PRO TIPS

Season: Fall-spring

Difficulty: Easy-moderate

Time needed: Day trip

- Indian Canyons has a per-person fee to enter, but it's worth it.
- Tahquitz Canyon has a separate entrance fee if you decide to go as well.
- Take extra water--you are in the desert.
- Go early in the day before it's hot and take lunch with you.
- Do not go into the dead palm fronds, even when they look like caves or huts--insects, bees, or small rodents can fall on you.
- As you hike, look for where the water comes out of the ground. Places where water seeps out of the ground are springs.
- The Andreas Canyon Loop will take you through the oasis to the spring where water feeds the oasis, then it loops gradually up the hill above the palm tree line to see the oasis from a new perspective.
- Another oasis you can visit in the Palm Springs area is the Coachella Valley Preserve. The cost is free, and has a fun boardwalk to view the first oasis and hiking trails to view a second oasis pond and surrounding area.

refreshing oasis

SHOW NOTES

An oasis is more than just water in the desert. It is the fertile area of land, full of life, that this water creates. Oases are important because they provide essential food and water for plants and animals. Throughout history, oases have served as places for travelers to rest and replenish food and water supplies. Some oases are also used as water sources for cities and agriculture.

The oases of Indian Canyons in Palm Springs have served as home to the Agua Caliente Band of Cahuilla Indians for thousands of years. The area provided them with abundant water so they were able to build complex communities with irrigation ditches, water reservoirs, dams and agriculture. They planted crops such as melons, beans, squash, and corn. Today, these beautiful, life-giving oases are listed on the National Register of Historic Places, preserving them for their historical significance.

VIDEOS AND RESOURCES

MY PLAYLIST

music, books, podcasts...

SUGGESTED JAM

Track: It's 1200 Miles From Palm Springs to Texas.

Artist: Dean Martin

MEET THE LOCALS

get to know the flora, fauna and features

CALIFORNIA FAN PALM

The California fan palm is the largest palm tree in the world. Its leaves are three to five feet long and fan-shaped. This palm produces edible black berries that have a large seed and a thin layer of fruit. Coyotes and birds eat the fruit and spread the seeds throughout the desert in their poop.

OASIS FRESH WATER

The water of the oasis is the source of life of all plants and animals around it. This water comes from underground aquifers (underground rock layers that hold groundwater) and springs. Palm trees protect the oasis from becoming polluted from winds carrying sand.

ARMORED STINK BEETLE

When the armored stink beetle is threatened, it will stand on its head and spray its predator with repellent chemicals. These insects eat decaying materials, such as fallen leaves and flower petals. They are active year round and hide in holes in the ground to escape the heat.

NARROWLEAF WILLOW

The narrowleaf willow is also known as the coyote willow. Native Americans used its smaller branches to make baskets and its bark to make string and rope. Its bark and leaves contain salicin (a chemical similar to aspirin) and is used to treat toothaches, stomach aches, and pain.

CALIFORNIA BARREL CACTUS

The California barrel cactus has long spines that give it shade. You can make different sounds by flicking these spines with your fingers. When there's no water, a barrel cactus gets thinner. Then, when rain falls, it will soak up water like a sponge and become plump again.

MY REVIEW

Write about your experience

TOP 5 HITS

1. Check out the Creature Chats. These are done in small, more personal feeling groups. Workers are knowledgeable and will answer questions.
2. Weigh yourself and family on the creature scale between the giraffes and rhinos.
3. Sketch or nature journal at the giraffe viewing area. This enclosure has a mix of animals to choose from.
4. Climb in large pots and explore at Village WaTuTu.
5. Visit the on site Tennity Wildlife Hospital and see an animal being cared for.

PRO TIPS

Season: Fall, winter, and spring when temperatures drop

Difficulty: Easy, but like most zoos, be prepared to walk

Time: Day trip

- Go to the zoo as early as possible, desert animals are most active before the heat of the day.
- The zoo is split into three main areas: North America, Africa, and Australia. Visit the Australian and North American Desert side first and do the scavenger hunt while everyone is full of energy.
- The Australian Adventures area lets you walk around the trail with wallabies and parakeets freely roaming around. You can sit on the large flat rocks and sketch them or even laugh with a laughing kookaburra.
- Take time to sketch or nature journal when kids are tired or asking for a snack.
- Walk to the car for lunch; the zoo is small, so it's not a long walk.
- The African Desert side has more shade. Do this on the second half of your day.

Giraffe!

SHOW NOTES

It can be tricky to see animals when visiting an actual desert. Most of the animal life will be hiding to stay out of the hot sun and avoid predators. You can see desert animals, though, at the Living Desert Zoo and Gardens. This unique place focuses on animals that live and survive in the North American, Australian, and African Deserts. The Living Desert Zoo works to preserve, conserve, and interpret the desert and all its varied animal and plant life. Here, you'll get the chance to connect with desert animals and plants. The "Animal Chats" at this zoo, for example, are fun, educational, and interactive (and by far the best we have seen at a zoo). Families are able to see the animals up close and ask any questions to trained knowledgeable workers. The zoo also offers many garden and hiking trails to explore, each focusing on a different plant ecosystem. When we go to the Living Desert Zoo and Gardens we are supporting conservation research, habitat protection, breeding programs, and education initiatives locally and around the world.

VIDEOS AND RESOURCES

MY PLAYLIST

music. books. podcasts...

SUGGESTED JAM

Track: Desert Sunrise

Artist: Brett Dennen

MEET THE LOCALS

get to know the flora, fauna and features

LIVING DESERT ZOO

MOUNTAIN LION

A mountain lion has large, specialized eyes that allow it to see in the dark. Its fur is sandy in color so it can stay camouflaged from its prey. When hunting, it pounces and bites its prey's neck so it can't get away. It eats eight to 10 pounds of meat a day to survive.

DESERT TORTOISE

The desert tortoise is a diurnal animal, meaning it is active during the day. It uses its strong forearms and tough nails to dig burrows where it can stay cool. When these tortoises drink, they store the water in their bladder. If needed, they can go up to one year without drinking.

KIT FOX

Kit foxes get all of their water from their prey. They can drink but don't need to. The pads of their feet are very hairy, which helps them walk on the hot desert floor and gives them traction on the sand. They also have very large ears that help hear rodents underground.

RATTLESNAKE

Rattlesnakes hibernate during the winter and are cold-blooded, meaning they rely on their surroundings to stay warm. They do best in temperatures between 70 and 90 degrees Fahrenheit. If the weather gets too hot or cold, they will die. They hide under rocks and in burrows when it's too hot.

CHUCKWALLA

A chuckwalla doesn't need to drink water; it gets all its water from the flowers, fruit, and leaves that it eats. When threatened, it will dive into a crack in the rocks and gulp air until its body inflates and becomes so wedged between the rocks that it cannot be pulled out.

MY REVIEW

Write about your experience

39

JOSHUA TREE

DATE

NATIONAL PARK

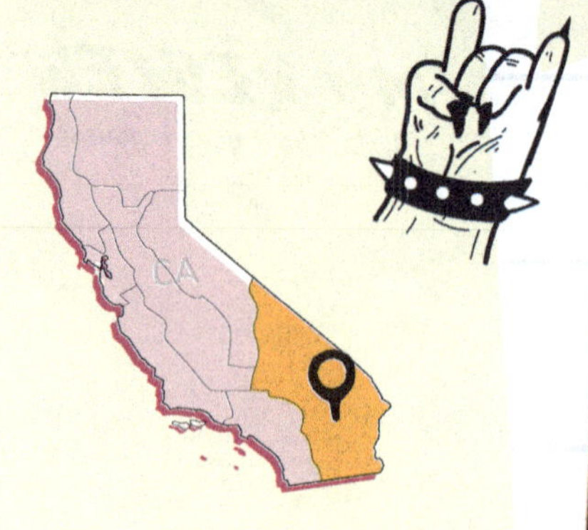

PRO TIPS

Season: Year round, but the most comfortable weather is Oct. - May.

Time: 1-2 days

Difficulty: Easy

- Download a night sky app for constellations before you go.
- Stop at a Visitor Center and get a map.
- There is no cell service in the park.
- Bathrooms are located at the Visitor Centers, campgrounds, and on the side of the road between Skull Rock and Keys View.
- Skull Rock is right next to the main road. Jumbo Rocks is the area directly behind it. Take your time and hike between and scramble on all the rocks. This is a great spot for kids.
- Bring one gallon of water per person in your car. This is the desert, and drinking water is not provided in the park.
- Bring an extra pair of pants for children who love to climb rocks. The monzogranite rocks and boulders are made up of large crystals that can easily break holes in their pants.

TOP 5 HITS

1. Scramble around Jumbo Rocks behind Skull Rock. Length is up to you.
2. Hike to Arch Rock and scramble on rocks (trail starts in White Tank Campground). .6 mile round trip.
3. Hike Hidden Valley. 1 mile loop.
4. Hike and sketch or nature journal at Barker Dam. 1.1 mile round trip.
5. Walk the boardwalk at Cholla Cactus Garden. .25 mile loop.

They call it a Joshua Tree

SHOW NOTES

With 790,636 acres of desert, Joshua Tree National Park is larger than the state of Rhode Island! Over 1.5 million people come to visit the park each year to hike the trails, camp under the stars, climb on rocks, birdwatch, walk through palm groves, paint, or just be inspired by the natural beauty of the desert. And, of course, to see Joshua trees.

The Joshua tree was named by Mormon immigrants in the mid-19th century. Legend tells us that these trees reminded the early pioneers of Joshua from the Bible, reaching up to the sky to pray. These twisty, spiky, Dr. Seuss-like plants are a sight to see—they grow up to 40 feet tall! Joshua trees grow an average of 1.5 to 3 inches per year. The Joshua tree is only found in the Mojave Desert and has two symbiotic relationships that are vital to its survival. Without the help of the yucca moth and a fungus called mycorrhizae, the Joshua tree would eventually disappear.

VIDEOS AND RESOURCES

MY PLAYLIST

music, books, podcasts...

SUGGESTED JAM

Track: Joshua Tree.
Artist: Rozzi

MEET THE LOCALS

get to know the flora, fauna and features

JOSHUA TREE

The Joshua tree is said to have been named by Mormon settlers because it reminded them of Joshua in the Bible reaching up to the sky to pray. It has a mutualistic relationship with the yucca moth, who pollinates the Joshua tree and lays its eggs on the flowers.

MOJAVE YUCCA

The Mojave yucca is also called the "Spanish dagger". Its leaves are evergreen succulents that grow only from a place called a rosette at the top of the tree. Native Americans used its leaves to build houses, sandals, rope, baskets, and bowstrings.

TEDDY BEAR CHOLLA

The teddy bear cholla has so many spines that it looks fuzzy. Do not touch a cholla cactus--the spines have hooks on them that are painful to take out. Chollas do not have seeds. Instead, wind and animals can break off small segments of cholla that will grow into whole new plants.

SKULL ROCK

Skull Rock looks like a giant skull. It isn't made of bone, though--it's made of granite. Over time, raindrops collected in small holes in the rock, slowly eroding pieces of it away. As more and more rock eroded away, two hollowed-out eye holes formed, giving it its skull-like shape.

DESERT COTTONTAIL

The desert cottontail rabbit's name comes from its white tail, which looks like a cotton ball. Keep an eye out for the animal's tracks, which look like the number seven. Not only can their four-inch ears hear danger, but they also release heat to keep the rabbit cool.

MY REVIEW ☆☆☆☆☆

Write about your experience

TOP 5 HITS

1. Climb the ladders in Ladder Canyon. Full loop, Ladder Canyon then returning through Painted Canyon 4.9 miles.
2. Enjoy the view above Ladder Canyon.
3. Find quartz in Big Painted Canyon.
4. Look at the many colored rocks in Big Painted Canyon, including zebra stripes!
5. Descend the ropes near the end of Big Painted Canyon (not too steep for kids).

PRO TIPS

Season: Oct. - April, when temperatures aren't so hot.

Difficulty: Moderate 4.5 mile loop, 967-foot elevation gain.

Time Needed: 3-4 hour hike with kids.

- Ladder Canyon is a slot canyon with ladders that allow you to climb up the dry waterfalls so you can keep exploring more parts of the slot.
- When you get to the top of Ladder Canyon, always stay on the trails that go to the right or straight. They will lead you down into Big Painted Canyon. Do not go left! It will take you on a long hike in the sun followed by a steep rope descent into another small slot canyon (not safe for little kids).
- Rock arrows made by volunteers will guide you clockwise and through the hike.
- Hike starts by hiking through a box canyon for .25 miles. The entrance to Ladder Canyon will be on your left and looks like a rock pile blocking the canyon. Don't be fooled; go in!
- Bring a four-wheel drive vehicle. Don't drive into the sand and park on a rocky area or you could get stuck.
- Don't leave valuables in your car--break-ins have been reported at the trailhead.
- Do not go after it rains as roads will be bad and flash floods may occur.
- You must be able to climb ladders to do this hike.
- Download the AllTrails trail map before you go (there is poor to no cell reception on hike).
- Bring lots of water and snacks!

SHOW NOTES

Mecca Ladder Canyon Hike is located in the heart of the Mecca Hills Wilderness Area on the active San Andreas Fault. The Mecca Hills were formed by the convergence (coming together) of the continental North American Plate and the oceanic Pacific Plate. The uplift of the continental plate has left raised sandstone layers of pink, red, purple, brown, and green mineral deposits that can be seen in Big Painted Canyon. Hiking through Ladder Canyon and Painted Canyon offers a slot canyon experience, stunning views, and the opportunity to see Painted Canyon and all its color!

As its name implies, the ladders of Ladder Canyon make this hike unique. Tucked into a beautiful slot canyon, they allow you to climb up dry waterfalls. The full loop is about 4.9 miles, so you'll need to bring snacks and plenty of water. You are also hiking in the desert, so plan for the hot weather and don't hike this area after it has been raining. Flash floods can damage the trails and ladders.

vertical cliff slot canyons

VIDEOS AND RESOURCES

MY PLAYLIST

music. books. podcasts...

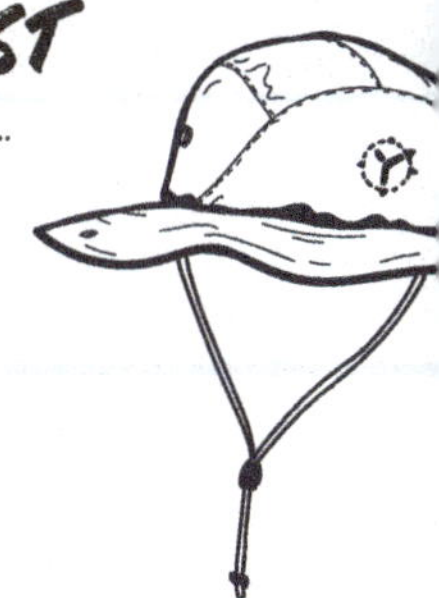

SUGGESTED JAM

Track: The golden state (featuring Eddie Vedder)

Artist: John Doe

MEET THE LOCALS

get to know the flora, fauna and features

CAIRNS

Cairns are stacks of rocks made by hikers to help them find their way back from a long hike in a new area. Don't make cairns for fun. Hikers can become lost if too many cairns are randomly made.

SLOT CANYON

Slot canyons are tall, narrow, windy canyons that are formed by water. Look closely at the base of the canyon walls. Do you see any evidence of water being in the area? The walls of the canyon are carved by rushing water carrying rocks that wear away and smooth the walls.

ARROWS MADE OUT OF ROCK

Arrows made out of rocks are made by volunteer hikers. These arrows exist to help visitors safely find their way through the windy paths. It could be easy to get lost without them. Make sure to have a map just in case the rain washes the arrows away.

OCOTILLO

The ocotillo is one of the tallest desert plants, growing up to 15 feet tall. It has long, shallow roots that spread in all directions. Red flowers grow on its stem tips in the spring. It has hundreds of little leaves that it sheds when there's a drought, then grows back when it rains.

DRY WATERFALL

Dry waterfalls are the skeletal remains of a waterfall. At Ladder Canyon, you can climb the dry waterfalls using ladders. During a rainstorm, water will flood the canyon, bringing the dry waterfall to life! As the rains stop, the water will evaporate, leaving the dry waterfall behind.

MY REVIEW

Write about your experience

41

DATE

ANZA-BORREGO DESERT STATE PARK

PRO TIPS

Season: Mid-Mar. to mid-May is the best time to see wildflowers (check the park website to see if there is a bloom this year)

Difficulty: Easy--longest hike is about one mile

Time Needed: Day trip

- Go to The Slot, Cactus Loop and any other hikes before you go to the Visitor Center or to see the sculptures. This will help you to beat the crowds and heat of the day.
- The Slot is a loop trail, instead of hiking the full loop, hike The Slot to its end then come back through it again to return to your car. The second part of the loop goes up to the top of The Slot in full sun and is not as fun for kids.
- Four-wheel drive and high clearance is needed on dirt roads, especially the road to the oases.
- Bring lots of water, food, and snacks; there are not many places to eat in Borrego Springs.
- Call the Wildflower Hotline to ask about this year's wildflower updates. (760) 767-4684 It lets you know if there is a bloom and where the bloom is located.
- Fill the gas tank before entering the park. Gas prices are higher in Borrego Springs.
- Download or print a park map before you go. The Visitor Center is in Borrego Springs in a central location, so you will drive past the many hikes, flowers and sculptures trying to get there.

TOP 5 HITS

1. Hike The Slot, .8 mile out and back.
2. Hike Cactus Loop Trail, .75 mile loop.
3. Drive to see all the sculptures (the Serpent "Dragon" is my favorite).
4. See the wildflower superbloom. This doesn't happen every year, call ahead and visit in the spring.
5. Take in the view at Fonts Point.

SHOW NOTES

For about 6,000 years, the Cahuilla, Cupeno, and Kumeyaay Native American lived in Anza-Borrego. Very little is known about them, but archaeologists have discovered that they did not use pottery or bows and arrows. Instead they used underground, rock-lined storage cysts to store food and they hunted with spears. These early people were also Nomadic and followed the food availability brought on by the seasons. Many archaeological sites with pictographs (rock paintings), petroglyphs (rock etchings), and mortars (grinding stones) have been found throughout Anza-Borrego. These sites are protected, and their locations are not shared with the public as a measure to preserve them.

There are many fun recreational opportunities in this area, such as hiking, slot canyon exploration, and four-wheeling, along with the chance to see giant sculptures and desert plants (including spectacular springtime wildflower blooms). Check out the cactus loop trail which is full of different types of cacti, succulents and other desert plant life. If you go in the spring, you can even see them flowering!

desert flowers

VIDEOS AND RESOURCES

MY PLAYLIST

music. books. podcasts...

SUGGESTED JAM

Track: Dani California

Artist: The Red Hot Chili Peppers

MEET THE LOCALS

get to know the flora, fauna and features

BARREL CACTUS

The barrel cactus has long spiky spines that give it shade and are okay for you to touch. You can make different sounds by flicking the spines with your fingers. When there's no water, a barrel cactus gets thinner. Then, when it rains, it will soak up water like a sponge and get plump again.

DESERT AGAVE

The desert agave stores water in its long, thick leaves. It has spikes on the edges and tips of its leaves for protection. There is a thick coating on its leaves that protect it from water loss and sunburn. Native Americans used to make rope, baskets, and sandals out of the leaves.

OCOTILLO

The ocotillo is one of the tallest desert plants, growing up to 15 feet tall! It has long, shallow roots that spread in all directions. Red flowers grow on the tips of its stems in the spring. It has hundreds of little leaves that it sheds when there's a drought then grows back when it rains.

DESERT DANDELION

The desert dandelion is an annual wildflower that grows back yearly after it rains. Its seeds have a seed inhibitor on them that needs to be washed off by rain before it can grow. Its flowers look like a bright yellow dandelion in your yard, but its leaves are thin and wiry-looking.

SAND SERPENT SCULPTURE

There are more than 130 sculptures by the artist Ricardo Breceda in Borrego Springs. Some, like the Sand Serpent, were created by the imagination of Breceda, but many others, like the Sabertooth Cat and Columbian Mammoth, were inspired by their fossils that were found there.

MY REVIEW

Write about your experience

42

TOP 5 HITS

1. Walk among the art structures at Bombay Beach. Drive around the outer homes to find the airplane!
2. Walk around Salvation Mountain.
3. Hike Rock Hill Butte, (a small volcano) 2 miles round trip.
4. Go birding. Watch out for burrowing owls peeking out of artificial burrows and pipes at the Sonny Bono Salton Sea National Wildlife Refuge.
5. See the fishbone sand at Salton Sea Recreation Area

PRO TIPS

Season: Best time is Oct.-May when it's not so hot.

Difficulty: Easy, short walks

Time Needed: Day trip

- Bring lots of water.
- Prepare to drive. It takes about 20 minutes getting from place to place.
- Bring enough food for the day, there are no food locations on the route.
- Explore with an open mind, ready to see a different world.
- All the art you will see on your trip including Salvation Mountain were made from repurposed wood and other materials. Some of which you might see in your trash or recycling.
- The Sonny Bono Salton Sea Wildlife Refuge is one of the better places for birding, including seeing a burrowing owl. Look at all the metal and plastic pipes near ditches and roads. Many pipes have been purposely placed as homes for the owls.
- Binoculars are a must for viewing birds; keep a close eye to see other wildlife like coyotes and bobcats near the birds.
- Contact the Sonny Bono Salton Sea National Wildlife Refuge to go on a free guided hike: (760) 348-5278
- All the power plants you will see are geothermal power plants, meaning they produce clean, renewable energy from steam built up in the earth.
- Salvation Mountain is great for kids to walk around.
- Sonny Bono Salton Sea National Wildlife Refuge has two small hikes; Red Hill Butte, 2 mile round trip, and the Hardenburger Trail through the duck ponds, .7 mile loop.

The Salton Sea

VIDEOS AND RESOURCES

SHOW NOTES

The Salton Sea was formed in 1905, when silt blocked the path of the Imperial Canal along the Colorado River, causing it to change course. Water from the Colorado River flooded into the Salton Sea for two years until the Southern Pacific Railroad fixed the canal and diverted the river back to the Imperial Canal.

In the 1950's, many people visited the new Salton Sea for sport fishing and vacationing and considered it to be the Riviera of the Americas. Shore and seabirds were also attracted to the area. Without the flow of fresh water from the Colorado River, the Salton Sea became more salty and polluted over time. Vacationers left the area, leaving buildings abandoned. As the salinity of the sea rose, many fish died, leaving only tilapia and desert pupfish in the sea. Thousands of sea birds still flock to the sea, making it an ideal place for birdwatching. If you look carefully at storm drains and plastic tubes near roads and ditches, you might even see a burrowing owl!

CALIFORNIA
US
10

SUGGESTED JAM

Track: Salton Sea

Artist: Josh Rouse

MEET THE LOCALS

get to know the flora, fauna and features

FISH BONE SAND

As the salinity of the Salton Sea rose, many species of fish died. Their bodies drifted to the beaches and decomposed, leaving behind their bony skeletons. Over time, these skeletons have been breaking down into boney sand particles.

GREAT BLUE HERON

The great blue heron hunts fish and other small water animals. They stand still looking into the water, and as their food comes near they will jab their long beaks into the water, stabbing their prey! When these birds fly, they tuck their long necks against their body in an "S" shape.

BROADLEAF CATTAIL

The broadleaf cattail's leaves look like thick, long grass. It can easily be recognized from its dense, brown spike that looks like a corn dog! When these spikes flower they become a white fluffy mass. Much of the plant, like the lower stalk and young flower spikes, is edible.

BURROWING OWL

Burrowing owls make their homes from small tunnels in dry, open areas. Unlike other owls, they will hunt grubs and small animals during the day (usually in the morning and evening). Over 70% of the burrowing owl population is found within the Salton Sea ecosystem.

THE DEATH SHIP

The Death Ship was created by artist Sean Guerrero for the yearly Bombay Beach Biennale. Many works of art have been created to draw attention to the Salton Sea and its need to be saved. This art challenges the world to find beauty in what is considered waste and to see the natural world in a new light.

MY REVIEW

Write about your experience

SOUTHERN CALIFORNIA

People come here for the sunshine and beautiful beaches but there is much more to it than that. Hike to spectacular white sandstone boulders of Ojai's Piedra Blanca, or head to Vasquez Rocks where you can climb on the tilted rock that has been violently exposed and shifted over the past 25 million years by the legendary San Andreas Fault. Take a getaway weekend at Bear Lake for quick easy access to slopes or time at the lake. Or head to Switzer Falls for a day hike to get out of the city. In the Santa Monica Mountains you can hike the historic Solstice Canyon followed by a relaxing time at the beach and bluffs of Malibu's Point Dume. Learn about the native Satwiwa tribe at Rancho Sierra Vista followed by a bike ride to the sea. Head further south and you can see and support animals on the brink of extinction at the world-class San Diego Zoo. Visit Torrey Pines State Reserve in San Diego for ocean cliff walks, long walks on the beach, amazing sunsets, and witness the rarest pine tree in North America. San Diego is also a great place to witness gray whales as they head up the California coast for the longest migration on the planet, an astonishing round trip of 12,000 miles.

TOP 5 HITS

1. Hike Piedra Blanca, 2.6 miles round trip.
2. Sketch plants and rock formations.
3. Climb and name the different rock formations. (What do they remind you of, an elephant, rhino?)
4. Swim in the swimming hole, .25 mile from parking.
5. Have a picnic at the swimming hole or at the picnic area by the parking lot.

PRO TIPS

Season: Open year round, best seasons are fall, winter and spring.

Difficulty: Moderate, 2.6 mile, 383ft. elevation gain

Time Needed: Day trip

- To get to the rock formations hike the Sespe Creek Trail till it reaches a T in the trail. Take a left at the T following the Piedra Blanca Trail. Get off the trail and explore as you reach the large white rocks. Look around so you can find the trail again when you want to leave.
- Listen for frogs croaking near the river. This trail crosses the Sespe River without a bridge, you will cross it by stepping on river rocks.
- The trail to the swimming hole is about .25 mile down the Sespe River Trail from the parking lot. It is on your left just before the signs that say no camping.
- Watch for rattlesnakes as you hike.
- You need an Adventure Pass or a National Parks Pass to park at the trailhead. You must purchase a pass before you go, you can't buy one there. Google- adventure pass Los Padres National Forest, to find locations that sell adventure passes.
- Restrooms are located at the trailhead and there is no running water, bring your own.
- This trail is mostly exposed with little shade, go early or late in the day to avoid the heat.
- Cool off in the swimming hole after your hike, it is a deep slow spot in the river, bring life vests if needed.

take a hike!

SHOW NOTES

Los Padres National Forest contains thousands of trails over mountains, through forests, and across beaches. The area of Piedra Blanca is located in Ojai, California, between the Sespe Wilderness, Hines Peak, and not too far from the Sespe Condor Sanctuary. The Sespe Wilderness area makes up the fourth largest roadless region remaining in the contiguous United States, making it even more special.

The rock formations in this area take on all kinds of different shapes and sizes. The white colored rocks look like various nature-made sculptures poking out from the green shrubbery. Many of the formations are made of sandstone and reveal a history of underlying geologic movement. The Piedra Blanca Trail follows along Sespe Creek and crosses a few other streams, providing opportunities to trek through riparian habitat and take a swim. Be sure to peer into the crystal-clear waters of Sespe Creek as you get a closer look: this is the last free-flowing, undamned river in southern California! It runs just over 30-miles through the wild and scenic California woodlands.

VIDEOS AND RESOURCES

MY PLAYLIST

music, books, podcasts...

SUGGESTED JAM

Track: Ojai

Artist: Ray Lamontagne

MIX TAPE

MEET THE LOCALS

get to know the flora, fauna and features

ARROYO TOAD

The small, stocky Arroyo toad is an endangered species. It has a V-shaped stripe on the top of its head, stretching eye to eye. They may be underground during the day or during harsh conditions, being mostly active at night (called nocturnal). Listen for their "uhh, uhh" call when near a river.

COTTONWOOD TREE

Cottonwood trees can grow quickly and reach gigantic sizes. All cottonwoods develop cotton-like strands around their seeds each June, a distinguishing feature. This tree "fluff" disperses seeds with the wind. These deciduous hardwoods lose their large, finely-toothed, triangle-shaped leaves each fall.

CREOSOTE BUSH

The creosote bush is a common shrub found in deserts. Locate this plant by looking for flexible green limbs with waxy, pointed leaves excellent for conserving water. On the plant, search for fuzzy white capsules - these are the shed seed-pods that develop from the yellow-petaled flowers.

RATTLESNAKE

Rattlesnakes hibernate during the winter and are cold blooded meaning they rely on their surroundings to stay warm. They do best in temperatures between 70 and 90 degrees Fahrenheit. If they get too hot or cold they will die. They hide under rocks and in burrows when it's too hot.

TURKEY VULTURE

Turkey vultures are the only scavenger birds that can't kill their own prey. They use their powerful beak to help force their heads into the body of dead animals. With the ability to identify scents over a mile away, these animals possess the strongest sense of smell of all birds.

MY REVIEW ☆☆☆☆☆

Write about your experience

44

DATE

RANCHO SIERRA VISTA-SATWIWA

SANTA MONICA MOUNTAINS NATIONAL RECREATION AREA

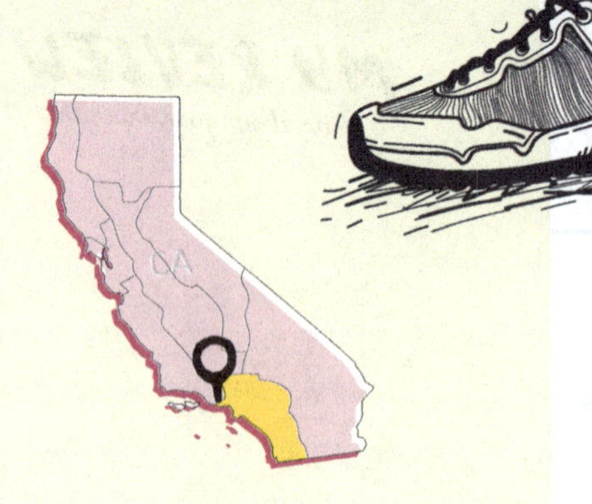

PRO TIPS

Season: Late winter and spring, waterfall dries up in the summer.

Difficulty: 3 miles round trip, moderate, uphill and not shaded trail.

Time Needed: 3-4 hours

- Bring lots of water and go early in the day. This trail is mostly exposed with little shade.
- From the Parking, take the trail next to the restrooms to the Satwiwa Native American Indian Culture Center and the trail to the Sycamore Canyon Waterfall. There is no visible trailhead sign.
- To get to the Sycamore Falls Trail, cross the small bridge that leads to the Satwiwa Culture Center and Chumash home. Take the trail that goes off to the right, directly after the bridge. It will lead you through the meadow then up and around the mountain to the falls.
- Going above the falls is dangerous for small children, the trail is narrow and involves rock ledges.
- Watch out for rattlesnakes, if you see one move away and wait for it to leave.
- Check out the native plant garden in front of the Satwiwa Native American Indian Culture Center.

TOP 5 HITS

1. Bike the Sycamore Canyon bike trail to the ocean. 8 miles to the beach.
2. Hike to Sycamore Canyon Waterfall, 3 miles round trip.
3. On your hike, sit at the bench that overlooks the area and take in the view, snack, and rest.
4. Go inside the Chumash Home replica.
5. Check out the Satwiwa Culture Center.

- Biking to the ocean through Sycamore Canyon is a popular thing to do. The Bike Trail is the wide paved trail by the Satwiwa Native American Indian Culture Center. If you take the bike trail to the ocean you will need someone in your party to drive to Sycamore Campground to pick you up. Park at Sycamore Cove Beach.
- The bike ride is 8 miles long. It is downhill and flat the whole way with 4-5 usually dry river crossings. The first 4 miles are paved then the last 4 miles are dirt. Mountain bikes are recommended. The first mile of downhill is steep so go slowly. After that it is flat with a slight downhill slope all the way to the beach.

SHOW NOTES

Standing proud and tall at 2,825 feet, Boney Mountain is one of the tallest mountains in California's Santa Monica Mountain Range. Parts of the Santa Monica Mountains were formed underwater, even though they're now the top of ridgelines!

Distinct protected lands converge in this area, including the Rancho Sierra Vista (Satwiwa) and the Point Mugu State Park. Historically, this place was home to the Chumash and Tongva/Gabrielino cultures. Sycamore Canyon lies in the western lands of this area, which served as an important trade route. The National Parks Service established the Satwiwa Native American Indian Culture Center and Natural Area nearby to honor the rich history here. View the waterfall in the Boney Mountain State Wilderness (best time to visit is the winter) and the Danielson Monument within the Satwiwa Loop and Hidden Valley Overlook areas. Biking or hiking from mountain to sea through the Sycamore Canyon is a local favorite.

Boney peak

VIDEOS AND RESOURCES

MY PLAYLIST

music, books, podcasts...

SUGGESTED JAM

Track: Ventura Highway

Artist: America

MEET THE LOCALS

get to know the flora, fauna and features

SHALE

Shale is a layered sedimentary rock, most often black or gray and sometimes varying to tan and red. It's made from mud that has been mixed with minerals and clay, resulting in flaky layers that have been used to make pottery, bricks, and tile.

CHUMASH (SATWIWA) HOUSE

A Chumash House, also called an 'Ap, is made of willow branches pounded into the ground and rounded into a dome structure. The Native American Chumash people created villages made up of these homes, which had holes at the top for air circulation.

SUGAR BUSH

The sugar bush (Rhus ovata) is an emerald-colored evergreen plant that grows into a shrub or small tree, often growing wider than it is tall. Pink and white flower clusters grow at the end of its branches, emitting a pleasant aroma.

DAMSELFLY

The damselfly comes in a variety of bright colors, often seen resting on vegetation. When resting, their four delicate wings are held in pairs vertically. They are beneficial predators that feast on insects, catching and holding them with their hairy legs during flight.

WESTERN FENCE LIZARD

The western fence lizard is black or brownish on top with an amazing blue belly patch. Males also have blue on their throats. They may be seen sunning themselves along trails, where they use super-fast reflexes to escape potential predators.

MY REVIEW ☆☆☆☆☆

Write about your experience

PRO TIPS

Season: Year round

Difficulty: Easy, 2.1 mile round trip

Time Needed: 2-3 hours

- Listen and locate all the birds you hear, woodpeckers and parrots are easier to spot when you follow the different bird sounds.
- Many of the plants along this trail are invasive species. They tend to be closer to the actual trail as their seeds come in on vehicles and shoes.
- The tropical plants at the ruins are not native to California, but are not considered invasive.
- Don't play in the river near the ruins. The river vegetation needs to recover from high use.
- If you look up the hill from the parking lot you will see a house that looks like Darth Vader.
- The waterfall is located behind the Tropical Terrace. Follow a short trail around the back of the terrace next to the river.
- Point Dume Cove Trail is located at the end of the paid parking lot at Point Dume State Beach. This is a short walk up to the cliff overlook. If you want to see more, keep following the trail to the top of the hill. Most people stop at the overlook and head back down.

TOP 5 HITS

1. Hike the trail to the ruins of The Roberts Ranch house (Tropical Terrace) and Solstice Waterfall, 2.6 mile round trip.
2. Explore the Tropical Terrace ruins and gardens.
3. See the Solstice Waterfall.
4. Drive 5 min away to Point Dume and walk up the Point Dume Cove Trail to see the view, .6 mile round trip to overlook, or 1.4 mile round trip to top of Bluff.
5. Play in the waves at Point Dume State Beach and enjoy the sand.

power hiking

SHOW NOTES

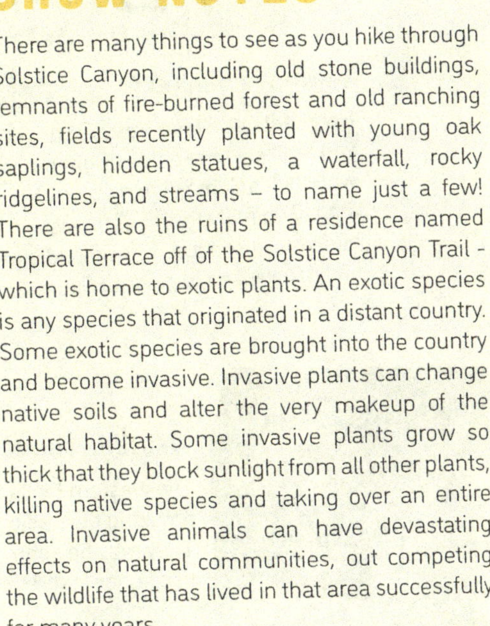

There are many things to see as you hike through Solstice Canyon, including old stone buildings, remnants of fire-burned forest and old ranching sites, fields recently planted with young oak saplings, hidden statues, a waterfall, rocky ridgelines, and streams – to name just a few! There are also the ruins of a residence named Tropical Terrace off of the Solstice Canyon Trail - which is home to exotic plants. An exotic species is any species that originated in a distant country. Some exotic species are brought into the country and become invasive. Invasive plants can change native soils and alter the very makeup of the natural habitat. Some invasive plants grow so thick that they block sunlight from all other plants, killing native species and taking over an entire area. Invasive animals can have devastating effects on natural communities, out competing the wildlife that has lived in that area successfully for many years.

Both the Rising Sun Trail and the Solstice Canyon Trail will lead you to a beautiful wooded waterfall and some interesting ruins. See how many native species you can recognize – ranging from oak and sycamore trees, to deer, quail, and bobcats.

VIDEOS AND RESOURCES

My PLAYLIST

music, books, podcasts...

SUGGESTED JAM

Track: Malibu

Artist: Hole

MEET THE LOCALS

get to know the flora, fauna and features

A DATE N.R.

NANDAY PARAKEET

Parakeets don't naturally occur in California, but you're likely to see this bright green parakeet with its black mask and beak, around the Malibu area. Originally from Southwestern Brazil, this bird was introduced or escaped into the wild and has naturalized in parts of Southern California.

WESTERN FENCE LIZARD

The western fence lizard is black or brownish on top with an amazing blue belly patch. Males also have blue on their throats. They may be seen sunning themselves along trails, where they use super-fast reflexes to escape potential predators.

ACORN WOODPECKER

The acorn woodpecker stores its nuts in tree holes they make called granaries. A granary tree can have up to 50,000 holes in it. They pack the nuts so tight that even squirrels can't pry them out.

TREE OF HEAVEN

The tree of heaven is a quick-growing invasive plant native to China. The plant has several names due to its stinky odor, mostly emitted from its yellowish flowers. Look for long, draping stems with green leaves arranged in pairs across from each other.

BLACK MUSTARD

Black mustard is an invasive plant that spreads rapidly and can grow as tall as 6 feet. Each plant is covered with thousands of bright yellow flowers that look pretty but produce thousands of seeds. These seeds can survive over 50 years buried deep in the soil.

MY REVIEW

Write about your experience

46

PRO TIPS

Season: Fall, winter, and spring (summer gets really hot)

Difficulty: Easy

Time Needed: 2-3 hours

- Bathrooms and Drinking fountains are Located in the Interpretive Center.
- When you are exploring Vasquez Rocks, have fun hiking, climbing and searching for your scavenger hunt items. Take time to talk about the items as you find them!
- There are more areas of the park to explore if you take the Horse Trail that leads up the hill just off of the Nature Trail. It will take you to even more large rocks and across the ridge for incredible views.
- Have fun exploring. This is a great place to say YES you can climb that! The rocks aren't as high or steep as you may think.
- Watch *The Flintstones* movie before or after you go, and look for Vasquez Rocks in the background. It's the backdrop for Fred Flintstone's House and some of the driving scenes.

TOP 5 HITS

1. Hike to and climb the main rock formation, 2 mile loop.
2. Check out the Interpretive Center and get a trail map.
3. Find the pictographs.
4. Take a picture with the Witches Hat formation on your head.
5. Climb and scramble on all the rocks you see.

natures movie set

SHOW NOTES

Rain, landslides, flooding and earthquakes brought vast amounts of soil, rocks, sand, and organic materials from the San Gabriel and Sierra Pelona Mountains down into the Solebad Basin over the past 25 million years. Over time, many layers of these sediments would form in the basin - creating lots of pressure and turning the deeper layers into sandstone.

Vasquez Rocks is located on the Elkhorn Fault (an offshoot of the San Andreas fault). Millions of years of earthquakes have caused the land to slide, causing the sandstone rock formations within Vasquez Rocks to lift out of the ground at 40–52-degree angles! Vasquez Rocks is the perfect place for rock explorers and fossil hunters of all ages. The constant moving and shifting of the earth has created lots of climbable and walkable rocks for families to explore. Over 62 movies and 112 television shows have featured the landscape of Vasquez Rocks!

VIDEOS AND RESOURCES

My Playlist

music. books. podcasts...

Suggested Jam

Track: California's Callin Me

Artist: Mike O'Rourke

MEET THE LOCALS

get to know the flora, fauna and features

PICTOGRAPHS

Pictographs are picture symbols that represent words or phrases. The pictographs you will see at Vasquez Rocks are replicas of real pictographs located in a protected area of the park. Try to find one of a snake and a sun!

GRINDING BOWL

Grinding bowls are smooth worn in areas in rocks that were used by the native Tataviam people to grind dried seeds and berries into flour. This can be found in the pictograph area.

DESERT VARNISH

Desert varnish are deposits of clay minerals which have been weathered out of the rock by the heat of the sun. These areas are harder and darker than the rock around them. Because they are harder they will take longer to break down than the rock around and below it.

CALIFORNIA JUNIPER

This juniper is an evergreen with bluish purple berries. The berries are edible but also bitter. They can be eaten raw, cooked or ground into a powder used for flavoring. The native Tataviam Tribe would dry and grind the juniper berries into a mush, which was used to make small cakes.

WITCHES HAT

This rock formation has become rounded and smoothed from wind, rain and being climbed upon. That's three types of weathering and erosion shaping this sandstone rock formation. If you look at it from the right angle it looks like a giant witches hat!

MY REVIEW

Write about your experience

PRO TIPS

Season: Spring and fall

Difficulty: Moderate, 4 mile round trip

Time Needed: 4-5 hours

- Purchase a parking pass before you drive to the trail. Park in the lower picnic area parking lots if possible.
- Google- adventure pass Angeles National Forest, to find locations that sell adventure passes.
- You can also park at the top parking lot next to the main road, but it will add .5 mile and 600 feet of elevation to your hike.
- Hike in the morning. Avoid the heat of the day.
- There are some small switchbacks going up that will appear on the right of the trail about 1 mile into your hike. They will lead you to the ridge section of the trail. If you keep walking on the trail past the switchbacks, it will shortly end at the top of a small waterfall.
- The last part of the hike goes along a high ridge with little shade. Bring lots of water and be careful with small children.
- Even if you decide not to finish the hike because of the high ridge, it is still worth the hike, the whole hike is beautiful! Especially the first part along the river before the ridge.
- Restrooms are located at the trailhead picnic area.

TOP 5 HITS

1. Hike the trail to Switzer Falls, 4 miles round trip.
2. Take time to explore along the riverbed.
3. Collect large acorn caps.
4. Climb and walk on fallen trees.
5. Snack or picnic on the rocks at the falls.

SHOW NOTES

Seasonal falls

Located within the San Gabriel Mountains is the 50-foot Switzer Falls, flowing through a woodland canyon. Perhaps the most interesting part about adventuring to this waterfall is that your journey will be upside down! From the beginning of the trailhead at the Switzer Picnic Area, the trail takes you downward for 650-feet, reaching the stream just below Switzer Falls.

Much of this hike will be traveling through a riparian zone – which is land surrounding a waterbody that is heavily influenced by the amount of water and moisture in this environment. Trees with roots that can withstand flooding and plants that prefer wet soils makeup the majority of this habitat. You may see abundant willows, alders, and cottonwoods. These productive riparian areas help mitigate impacts from flooding, provide food and cover for wildlife, and maintain water quality by acting as a filter and buffer against pollution.

VIDEOS AND RESOURCES

MY PLAYLIST

music, books, podcasts...

SUGGESTED JAM

Track: In California

Artist: Neko Case

MEET THE LOCALS

get to know the flora, fauna and features

WESTERN WHIPTAIL LIZARD

The western whiptail is a brown-and-black checkered lizard that rarely reaches 12-inches in length at maximum. Most of its body is tail, which the lizard can cast-off if attacked by a predator for a better chance at escaping danger! It takes a lot of energy, but the tail eventually can grow back.

CALIFORNIA FUSCHIA

California fuschia is often the only native flowering plant during the height of California summers. It produces beautiful red flowers both in summer and in fall. The long, thin flowers are very attractive to hummingbirds. This shrub grows best in full sun.

WESTERN GRAY SQUIRREL

Western gray squirrels are excellent at jumping and climbing. They communicate by making sounds and body movements. In the fall, they may "cache" or hide a variety of food, often acorns, for winter food. Many caches are never found and may sprout into young oak trees.

COAST LIVE OAK

Coast Live Oak trees have a broad, shrubby appearance with smooth green toothed leaves. It absorbs moisture from fog along the coast during dry periods. The plant produces flowers in spring and attracts a variety of birds and butterflies.

ALDER TREES

Alder trees commonly grow near water and in riparian areas. This tree is related to birches and in the right conditions grows quickly, sometimes close to two feet in a year! It can be recognized by the "eye" patterns on its white bark.

MY REVIEW ☆☆☆☆☆

Write about your experience

48

DATE

BIG BEAR LAKE

Season: Spring and fall

Difficulty: Moderate, 2 mile round trip with 700 ft. elevation gain.

Time Needed: Day trip

- Google- adventure pass San Bernardino National Forest, to find locations that sell adventure passes.
- Trail parking is on the main road next to the lake. The trail head is a short walk down the road at a road bend, be careful when walking down and crossing the road.
- It is a steep hike, but it is still fun with small children. There are lots of rocks to play on ¾ of the way up.
- Castle Rock looks like a large rock face from the trail. It is the only large rock face you will see on this trail.
- When you are almost to the Castle Rock formation you will reach a fun area to climb rocks and explore. The formation is less than .25 mile past this area. Keep following the rock tower trail markers to get there.
- The trail up to Castle Rock continues on past the Castle Rock formation in a switchback going up and to the left. Don't go up to the left. Instead hike around on the rocks to the right, around the back of Castle Rock and find the easy path up the rock formation. The top offers the best view of Big Bear Lake available!

1. Hike Castle Rock Trail, 2.7 miles round trip. Climb Castle Rock and enjoy the view.
2. Ski or snowboard Big Bear Mountain in the winter.
3. Paddleboard or Kayak around Boulder Bay Park.
4. Picnic at Ski Beach Park.
5. Visit the Big Bear Discovery Center.

- There is a kayak rental store right next to Boulder Bay Park. (Big Bear Lake Kayaks) They put the kayaks on rollers so you can walk them to the lake. You don't need a truck to transport a kayak.
- Big Bear Lake requires kayak permits to go on the lake. Ask the kayak rental for information.

best view of the lake

SHOW NOTES

The native Serrano culture called it "Pine Place," and it wasn't until 1883 that a rock dam was constructed to flood the area that forms Big Bear Lake. Before this, the surrounding mountains had been popular for logging and gold mining. In fact, gold mining is what initially attracted settlers to the immediate area – pushing the local population over 1,000 individuals in the 1860's.

Today, the lake itself is known for an abundance of fish, and the surrounding area is popular in all four seasons for activities ranging from skiing and snowboarding to hiking and mountain biking. Big Bear Lake sits at an elevation of 7,000-feet and is about eight miles long. Towards the western end of the Lake, directly across from Fisher Cove, is the beginning of Castle Rock Trail. This is a steep, rocky hike that ends in panoramic views over the lake and nearby peaks. The exciting climb, coupled with great views and a beautiful forested trail, has made this hike one of the most popular in the San Bernardino National Forest.

VIDEOS AND RESOURCES

MY PLAYLIST

music, books, podcasts...

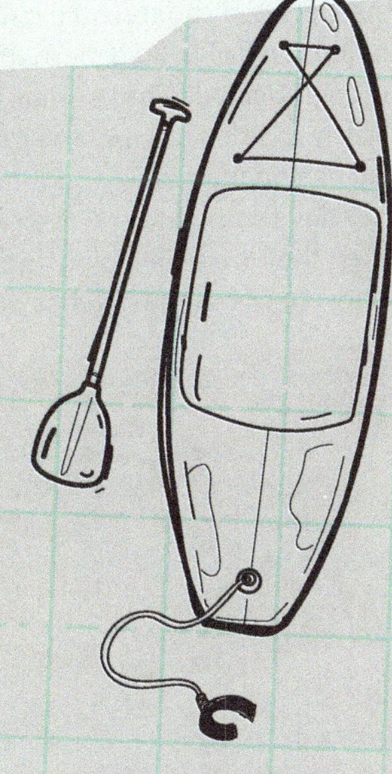

SUGGESTED JAM

Track: Big Bear

Artist: Steah

MEET THE LOCALS

get to know the flora, fauna and features

BUSH CHINQUAPIN

California's Bush Chinquapin has longish green leaves and develops round, spiky, burr-like green flowers in summer. This shrub grows slowly, reaching up to seven feet, and can live for a long time. It prefers rocky slopes and sandy soils. It serves as a host plant to up to ten species of butterflies and moths.

LODGEPOLE CHIPMUNK

The active lodgepole chipmunk has stark white stripes on the face and back. Females are larger than males, and the species occurs only in California and Nevada. They eat a variety of foods - those which aren't digested, like spores and seeds, are then dispersed around the forest, serving an important ecosystem role.

COMMON SAGEBRUSH LIZARD

The common sagebrush lizard is active during the day (called diurnal) from March through October. These small lizards are mostly mottled tan, but males have blue patches on their belly and throat. Females may have some blue on their bellies, and when they are developing eggs, they may show red or orange patches of color.

GREENLEAF MANZANITA

Manzanita is Spanish for little apple. A manzanita can be a small tree or large shrub and was named after its small red berries that resemble little apples. Its seeds will fall to the ground and remain dormant for years till a fire comes and cracks them open.

JEFFREY PINE

Jeffrey pines are closely related to ponderosa pines. One way to tell them apart is by their cones. The barbs at the end of the cone scales point inward instead of outward, so Jeffrey pine cones aren't prickly to touch. An easy way to remember this is by repeating the phrase "gentle Jeffrey and prickly ponderosa."

MY REVIEW

Write about your experience

49

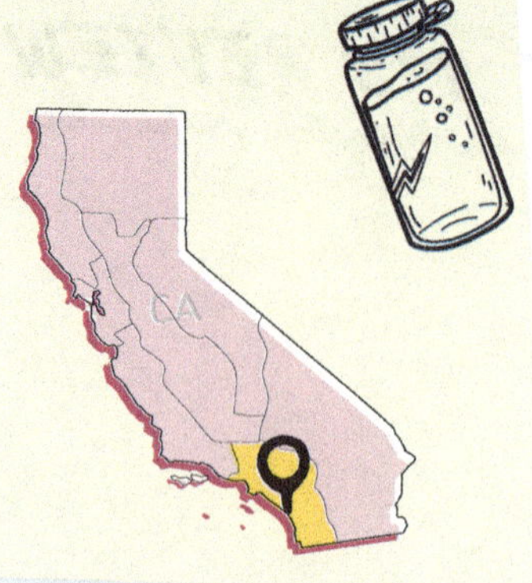

PRO TIPS

Season: Year round in SoCal.

Difficulty: Easy

Time Needed: Day trip

- Oceanside Strand Beach and City Beach have free street parking two streets away from the beach. You can also drop your family at the beach then go park the car. There is a small drop off loop at the intersection of Surfrider Way and The Strand N.
- Oceanside Harbor Beach has a paid parking lot, and is where you can take surf lessons.
- Watch out for seagulls, they are not shy and will take your food, even out of your hands.
- Use lots of sunblock, you can burn even on a cloudy day
- Good beginner surfing beaches in SoCal; Silverstrand-Oxnard, Mondos Beach- Ventura, Bolsa Chica- Huntington Beach, Harbor Beach and The Strand- Oceanside, Doheny State Beach- Dana Point, Dogpatch- San Onofre.
- If you are at a beach near an estuary, shuffle your feet when you're in the water to scare off rays. FYI: At Bolsa Chica near Huntington Beach the lifeguards have a sting treatment area at the main lifeguard building.
- If you are stung by a ray, soak your sting in hot water (As hot as you can handle) for 1 hour or until the pain stops. Some stings require a doctor visit for antibiotics.

TOP 5 HITS

1. Boogie Board
2. Surf
3. Run in and out of the waves
4. Picnic and build sand castles
5. Throw a frisbee or football back and forth in the shallow water.

Surfs up dude!

SHOW NOTES

Southern California is blanketed with beautiful beaches, ranging from calm inlets and refuges to action-packed tourist destinations. Oceanside Harbor Beach rests on the western side of a small peninsula, situated between the Pacific Ocean and a sliver of saltwater known as South Harbor. This area provides a wonderful place to play in the sand and learn how to surf the waves!

At Oceanside Harbor Beach, visitors can find numerous sea shells and may even catch a glimpse of seals or sea lions basking in the sunshine. The soft sand of California's beaches is most often made up of silicon dioxide in the form of quartz mixed in with some feldspar. While quartz is usually white or clear, feldspar is a pale brownish colored mineral. This combination of minerals gives Southern California its beautiful light brown sand. Whichever beach you decide to visit, there are so many activities to enjoy and nature to experience.

VIDEOS AND RESOURCES

MY PLAYLIST

music, books, podcasts...

SUGGESTED JAM

Track: California Girls

Artist: The Beach Boys

MEET THE LOCALS

get to know the flora, fauna and features

OCEANSIDE HARBOR BEACH

SEAGULL

Seagulls are white seabirds with dark wingtips, a strong body, and webbed feet. They are intelligent animals that can steal food from other birds, animals and from humans (like a sandwich straight out of kids' unsuspecting hands). They can also drink seawater.

PACIFIC SAND CRABS

These small Pacific sand crabs are great at burrowing into the sand to escape predators, which are a variety of seabirds. At the beach as the waves retreat out to sea, look for "V" shapes left in the sand. This just might be a sand crab filter-feeding on plankton and detritus.

SURFERS

Surfers may be solitary or in groups, either sitting, lying, or standing on a surfboard. These people are enjoying the sport of riding a wave towards the shore, carefully balancing on a specially made ocean-going surfboard. They're often seen floating atop the ocean water, waiting on a wave to ride.

CALIFORNIA MUSSEL

The California mussel will shut its shell tightly when it is exposed to air. When it is underwater it cracks its shell open and releases little cilia (hairs) that will bring in water and food. California mussels glue themselves to rocks by secreting byssal fluid that gets hard in sea water.

BROWN PELICAN

Brown pelicans have a gular pouch attached under their beak that they use as a net when catching fish. They dive quickly into the water at high speeds to catch its prey and can also scoop it out while swimming across the water's surface.

MY REVIEW ☆☆☆☆☆

Write about your experience

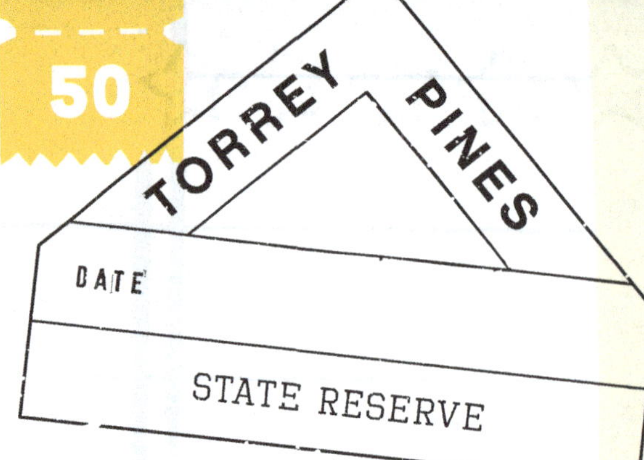

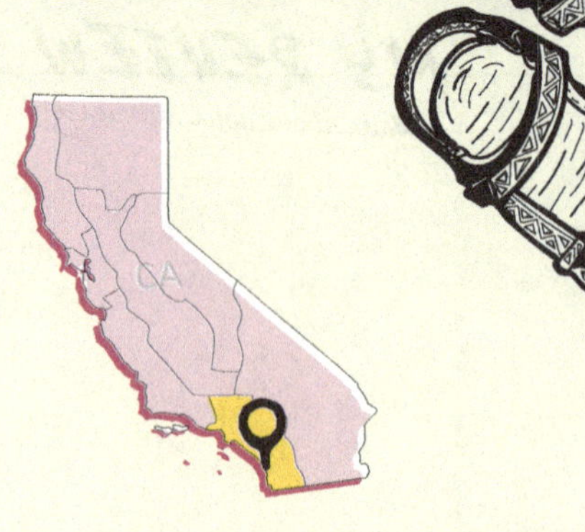

PRO TIPS

Season: Year round at low tide, it is hard to find parking in the summer

Difficulty: Easy, some steps with rails to get down to the beach, mostly sandy flat trails.

Time Needed: Day trip, hiking and beach day

Go at low tide to be able to go down to the beach. You cannot walk on the beach at high tide, the water hits the cliffs.

- Bring a hat or sunblock, the main trails are not shaded.
- Follow the road up the hill after you enter the state reserve to reach the trailhead parking lots.
- Check out the Visitor Center by the Torrey Pines Beach Trail parking lot, and get a trail map. There is a large sign with the trail name.
- Go in the morning to avoid crowds and find parking.
- Don't stand directly below the cliffs, people have died from eroding pieces of cliff falling on them, it's not safe.
- Bathrooms are located at the Visitor Center.

TOP 5 HITS

1. Hike the Beach Trail ¾ mile one way to the beach.
2. Check out Yucca Point along the Beach Trail.
3. Play at the beach and admire the colorful layered sandstone cliffs.
4. Find mussels and anemones on the large flat rock at the beach.
5. Hike Guy Fleming Trail, .8 mile loop. For large Torrey pines and ocean views.

SHOW NOTES

Spanish explorers named this area the "Point of Trees" because they used the trees as landmarks to help navigate their journeys. By the 1800s, however, the trees were cut and land cleared to make room for cattle grazing. Years later, 395 acres of Torrey Pines was donated by journalist Ellen Browning Scripps and set aside as a protected public park. Now the 2,000-acre reserve is home to about 300 endangered species of plants including the Torrey pine.

Winding, sandy hiking trails take you to overlooks of plant and animal life and amazing ocean views. Visiting at low tide is a great way to experience tide pool creatures and see the ancient 45-million-year-old rainbow-like sandstone cliffs! The entire reserve is located on distinct layers of ancient sandstone. Most fossils are found in sedimentary rocks since they are not created by magma or heat, which can destroy fossils. Be sure to visit the beach and experience the ancient sandstone layering by looking up at the cliffs.

VIDEOS AND RESOURCES

long walks on the beach

MY PLAYLIST

music. books. podcasts...

SUGGESTED JAM

Track: California Soul

Artist: Marlena Shaw

MEET THE LOCALS

get to know the flora, fauna and features

TORREY PINES

TORREY PINE

Torrey pines are only found at Torrey Pines State Reserve and on Santa Rosa Island. The pines growing on the sandstone cliffs are dwarfed and snarled by the wind and salty air. The pines that are in inland areas sheltered from these elements grow taller and more upright.

BLACK SAGE

The black sage has oval leaves that look like small green tongues up close. It grows larger leaves in the wet season and smaller leaves that reduce transpiration, water loss, in the dry season. Rub a leaf between your finger and smell, what does it remind you of?

LAYERED CLIFF FORMATIONS

Torrey pines cliffs are made up of 4 layers of sandstone formations dating 48 million to 400 thousand years ago. The oldest and lowest layer is the Delmar followed by Torrey Sandstone, Lindavista and Baypoint formations. The exposed layers can be seen looking at the cliffs from the beach.

COASTAL BARREL CACTUS

The coast barrel cactus is usually wider than it is tall. It only grows up to 12 inches tall. Its green flesh is shaped in ribs and is covered in long reddish spines. Its flesh, flower buds, and fruits can be used for food. Its flesh could also be pounded for drinking water!

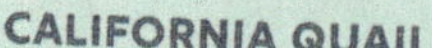

CALIFORNIA QUAIL

The California quail is the state bird of California. It has a small group of six feathers, shaped like a comma, on their head called a topknot. They spend most of their time on the ground and can fly to avoid predators such as coyotes and snakes. They live in groups called a covey.

MY REVIEW ☆☆☆☆☆

Write about your experience

51

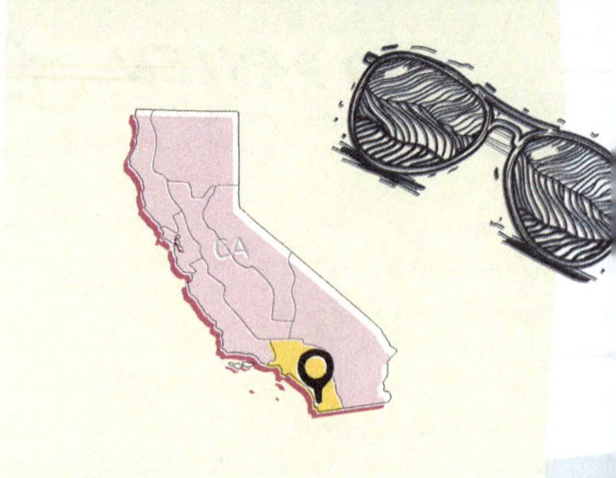

PRO TIPS

Season: Year round

Difficulty: Easy

Time Needed: Day trip

- Before you go make a plan to see everyone in your family's favorite animal.
- See as many wildlife encounters and presentations as possible and learn from professionals.
- Ask all questions that come to you, who better to ask than someone who works with the animals every day.
- Take your nature journal and sketch your favorite animals and what you learn about them.
- The zoo is huge, ride the kangaroo bus to your next location if you get tired, it's part of your paid admission to the zoo.
- You can bring food into the park, but you need to carry it with you at all times, no coolers allowed, backpacks are OK to bring.

TOP 5 HITS

1. Listen to a wildlife care specialist talk about the animals at the Wildlife Encounters.
2. Watch a polar bear swim in the Northern Frontier.
3. Gaze upon the largest tortoise you'll ever see in the Discovery Outpost.
4. Wander through the jungle along Monkey Way and Treetops Way.
5. Find your favorite animal and sketch it.

SHOW NOTES

The San Diego Zoo is home to over 12,000 animals, including over 650 different species spread out over 100 acres of Balboa Park. Be sure to visit the rarest creatures - those that are threatened or endangered in the wild – you'd probably never, ever see otherwise. Just by visiting the San Diego Zoo you are helping endangered animals, as a portion of your ticket cost goes to helping animals all across the world.

As you travel through this experience, take moments to stop and watch some of your favorite zoo residents. Can you notice things about them that may help them survive in the wild? Every animal has certain traits that allow them to thrive in their habitat. Some of these can be seen in the way an animal acts and moves (called behavioral adaptations). Does your favorite animal build a den, migrate during different seasons, or have a way of scaring off predators? These are examples of behavioral adaptations that help the animal survive.

VIDEOS AND RESOURCES

best zoo ever!

MY PLAYLIST

music. books. podcasts...

SUGGESTED JAM

Track: San Diego Zoo

Artist: The 6THS

BASS TO THE BONE

MEET THE LOCALS

get to know the flora, fauna and features

RING-TAILED LEMUR

The ring-tailed lemur lives in groups of around 30 lemurs and works as a team to stay safe and find food. A group of lemurs is called a "conspiracy". They have developed lower teeth that stick out and can groom fur like a comb.

RED PANDA

The red panda is nocturnal (active at night) and spends their time alone in trees. Their long tail helps them balance and stay warm. They have a small body that helps them climb and large wrist bones that act as thumbs for climbing down trees headfirst and grabbing food.

POLAR BEAR

Polar bears have black skin and transparent hair that looks white. They use their large paws to dig dens to protect themselves and cubs from the cold. They are also strong swimmers and spend up to %50 of their time hunting.

AFRICAN ELEPHANT

This is the largest land animal on the planet! They live in herds led by a female, called matriarchs. Their digestive system doesn't digest all of the food so they eat a lot, around 200 lbs. of food a day, and are constantly pooping out dung that helps new plants to grow.

ORANGUTAN

In the wild, orangutans use tools such as sticks to extract insects and honey to eat. They are critically endangered (extremely high risk of extinction in the wild) mostly because humans are destroying the forests that they live in order to produce palm oils.

MY REVIEW

Write about your experience

PRO TIPS

Season: Gray whales in the winter. Gray whales, fin whales, humpback and possible blue whales in the spring. Blue whales in the summer. Humpback and fin whales in the fall. Dolphin varieties year round.

Difficulty: Easy

Time Needed: Day trip

- We recommend https://nextlevelsailing.com in San Diego Bay. This ship switches to sail power as you hit the open sea to reduce noise pollution.
- Keep an eye on smaller children; the Yacht America sailing ship from Next Level Sailing has ropes but no solid rails.
- Kids will like sitting in the sunken seating by the captain at the back of the ship.
- Bring layers, the ride can become hot or chilly as the ship sails out to sea.
- Watch for white water spraying, it's the first thing you'll see when a whale is nearby.
- If you see a whale or sea life, point and holler and the captain will take you to it.
- The ship offers a light snack and beverages while you are on board.

TOP 5 HITS

1. Climb aboard the ship and look for whales.
2. Spot other sea life like dolphins, sea lions, and shorebirds.
3. Listen to whale presentations by ship staff or captain.
4. Sit back, snack and take in the views.
5. Ask a lot of questions about sea life and the ship.

WALKMAN

a whale of a time!

SHOW NOTES

Of all the animals on earth, gray whales undertake the longest migration, traveling up to 12,000-miles on a long-distance trek from their birthing lagoons in the warm waters of Mexico, to the cold food-rich waters of the northern arctic seas. The whole trip takes almost three months each way. And at a length around 40-feet, weighing a whopping 60,000 pounds – imagine the fuel and energy required to undertake this important migration!

There are hazards on this journey, including noise pollution, ship strikes and entanglement, and plastic pollution, to name a few. Since whales rely so heavily on sounds that transmit through the water, noise pollution is extremely problematic for navigating a successful migration and for locating prey. If your group decides to book a whale watching cruise, try to select a reputable expedition that uses a sailboat to reduce underwater noise. There are many locations to see migrating whales from land using binoculars; Cabrillo National Monument or Bluffs at Torrey Pines State Reserve are great options. For more locations across the state of California, visit https://thewhaletrail.org.

VIDEOS AND RESOURCES

MY PLAYLIST

music, books, podcasts...

SUGGESTED JAM

Track: Pretty Girl from San Diego

Artist: The Avett Brothers

MEET THE LOCALS

get to know the flora, fauna and features

SEA LIONS

Sea lions are mammals with large front flippers that propel them in the water and can be used to walk on land. They are a brownish-tan color and have small ear flaps. They eat fish, squid and octopus. They make loud noises that are similar to a lion's roar.

AMERICAN WHITE PELICAN

Pelicans have a gular pouch under their beak that they use as a net when catching fish. They can dive quickly into the water at high speeds to scoop prey while swimming across the water's surface. Their feet also have four webbed toes instead of three like most other water birds.

COMMON DOLPHIN

There are two species of common dolphin; a short beaked common dolphin and a long beaked common dolphin. They both have a dark back, a white underside and an hourglass light gray pattern on their sides. All dolphins are mammals and breathe air through a blowhole on top of their head.

SAILBOAT

A sailboat is a boat that has sails. A sailboat usually has two sails, a mainsail and a head sail, but can also have more. The front of the sailboat is called the bow and the back is called the stern. Sailboats use the wind to fill their sails and push them through the water.

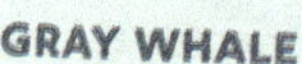

GRAY WHALE

Gray whales have dark gray bodies covered in white patterned scars left from parasites that hang on their bodies. They have baleen instead of teeth that they use to filter amphipods out of the water. They are mammals and have a double blowhole that they use to breathe air.

MY REVIEW ☆☆☆☆☆

Write about your experience

INDEX

PHOTOGRAPHY CREDITS

All photos by authors except for the following:

FLICKR

Esther Lee
Joshua Tree VII, 167

Judy Gallagher
Yucca Moth VII

George G Meade Public Affairs Office
Water Bottles VII

Alex Beattie
Hidden Valley VII

Don Graham
Forest, Sierra Nevada VIII
Desert Scrub,
Joshua Tree NP VIII

Justin Meissen
Coastal Sage Scrub VIII
California Grasslands IX

Mike McBey
Montane Meadows VIII
Crystal Crag 128
Half Dome Closeup
Yosemite 117

Jim Morefield
Alpine, Phlox IX
Bush Chinquapin205

Bureau of Land Management
RV, Alabama Hills IV
Oak Woodland IX
Roosevelt Elk 13
Black Cliffs 21
Ladder Canyon 170
Dry Waterfall 171

David Prasad
Chaparral IX

Matthew Dillon
Riparian Corridor X
Kings Canyon 132
Hoodoo 147

USFWS Pacfic Southwest
wetland X

Pacific Southwest Forest Service
Big Leaf Maple X

Tom Hilton
Western Dog Violets XI

John Rusk
Matilija Poppy XI
Pacific Aster XI
Sugar Bush 189

Neeta Lind
Coastal Redwood 5

Benny Mazur
Tadpole 5

Bureau of Land Management Oregon and Washington
River Rock 5
Gooseneck Barnacles 61, 87
Western Fence Lizard 193

Peter Linehan
Redwood Sorrel 5, 53

Kirt Edblom
Fern Canyon 8
Patricks Point State Park 16

Brian Bollman
Five Finger Fern 9

brewbooks
Lady Ferns 9

Brian Gratwicke
Ensatina 9

Born1945
Northern Red-legged Frog 9

Erik Fitzpatrick
Wavey Leaved Cotton Moss 9

Scott Edmunds
Banana Slug 13

Forest and Kim Starr
Sword Fern 5, 13, 53
Eucalyptus Seeds 49
California Fan Palm 159

David Berry
Octopus Tree 13

Jerry Kirkhart
Green Anemone 17, 61
Nudibranch Sea Lemon 17, 71
Gumboot Chiton 17
Purple Sea Urchin 61
Long Billed Curlew 67
Elephant Seal Pup 83
California Fuschia 201

Theo Crazzolara
Hermit Crab 17

Barb Ignatius
Purple Sea Star 17

Jay Cross
Shelter Cove 20

Tristan Ferne
Mussel 21, 209

David Goehring
Poison Oak 21

Joe Pell
Seagull 21, 209

Kuhnmi
Black Sand 21

Moonjazz
Russian River 24

Amit Patel
Merganser 25
Lava Flow 31
Mudpot 43
Fumarole 43

Tim Parker
Black Crowned Night Heron 25

Renee Grayson
Great Egret 25

Hari K Patibanda
Perigrine Falcon 25

Dick Culbert
Water Primrose 25

Jon Evans
Hydrophobic Bacteria 31

Sodai Gomi
Petroglyph Point 31
Turks Turban 147

Tenebboy
Lavacicles 31

Terry White
Indian Paintbrush 31

David Wood
Burney Falls 34

Wendy Cutler
Indian Rhubarb 35

Peter Stevens
Ponderosa Pine 35

Becky Matsubara
Golden-Mantled Ground Squirrel 129
Wild Turkey 53
Burrowing Owl 179
California Quail 213

California Department of Fish and Wildlife
Columbian Black-tailed Deer 35

Trevor Bexon
Burney Rainbow 35

psyberartist
Shasta Caverns 38
Stalactite Shasta 39, 113

Chris Luczkow
Stalagmites 39, 113

Ray_Explores
Column Shasta 39
Sutro Baths 57

James St. John
Basalt 35
Soda Straws 39, 113
Thermophilic Bacteria 43
Cave Bacon 39, 113
Cave Popcorn 113
Moro Rock 137

Don DeBold
Lassen, Bumpass Hell 42

Larry Lamsa
Corn Lily 43

Katja Schulz
Wolf Lichen 43

Dennis Jarvis
Point Reyes Lighthouse 48

Brandon Levinger
Tule Elk 48, 49

Caducosity
Miwok Loklo Village 49

Joshua Tree National Park
Turkey Vulture 49, 185

Bri Weldon
California Bay Laurel Tree 53
Sugar Bush 189
Coyote Brush 83

daveynin
Cypress Tree Tunnel 49
Purple Sand 75
Giant Sequoia 109
Mark Twain Stump 133
General Sherman 136
Fire Burn 137
Castle Rock Trail 204

H-wang
Lands End 56

Allie Caulfield
Redwood Burl 53
Mile Lighthouse 57
Heart Rock 57
Natural Bridges 60

Verygreen
Golden Gate Bridge 57

George Williams
Labyrinth 57

Beatrice Murch
Chiton 61

Jasmin Hunter
Periwinkle 61

NOAA National Ocean
Elkhorn Slough 66

Seabamirum
Owl Boxes 67

Don Loarie
Narrowleaf Willow 159
Coast Live Oak 67, 201

sfbaywalk
Pickleweed 67, 143

Andy Reago & Chrissy McClarren
Acorn Woodpecker 67, 193

Diana Robinson
Monterey Bay Aquarium 70

James Brooks
Sea Otter 71

Q Phia
Brittle Star 71

Steve Jurvetson
Giant Pacific Octopus 71

crudmucosa
California Moray 71

Henrique Pinto
Big Sur 74

Ravin
Mcway Falls 75

docentjoyce
Bixby Creek Bridge 75
Montaña de Oro State Park 86

Juan Alberto Garcia Rivera
Keyhole Arch 75

Oliver.dodd
Pinnacles NP 78

USFWS Pacific Southwest Region
California Condor 75, 79
Island Fox 95
Anza-Borrego 174
Arroyo Toad 185

Edward Rooks
Chamise 79

Hat4Rain
Spire Pinnacles Sentry 79

Fruit
Holly Leaf Cherry 79

Edward Rooks
Chamise 79

Ken Lund
Talus Cave 79
Channel Islands NP 94
Ojai 184

Bureau of Land Management of California
Elephant Seal 82

Greg Schechter
Elephant Seal Bull 83

Mark Gunn
Elephant Seal Male, Juvenile 83
Black Tailed Jackrabbit 147

bgwashburn
Elephant Seal Female 83
Nigel
Oyster Catcher 95
Jason Hollinger
Fuchsia Flowered Gooseberry 87
oliveoligarchy
Soap Plant 87
Linda Tanner
Lined Shore Crab 87
Lodgepole Chipmunk 125, 205
Anne Adrian
California Buckwheat 87, 147
Joshua Green
Lizard Mouth Rock 90
Orin Zebest
Tafoni 91
Richard Carmichael
Wind Caves 91
Pedro
Santa Cruz Island 91
Vahe Martirosyan
Our Lords Candle 91
Andrey Zharkikh
Greenleaf Manzanita 91, 133, 205
Horsetail 105
Silver Puff 151
John Game
Santa Cruz Island Live Forever 95
Ed Bierman
Garibaldi 95
Linking Tourism & Conservation
Giant Kelp 95
sam may
Lake Tahoe Kayak 100
Fannette Island 101
Andy Morffew
Belted Kingfisher 101
Jonathan Cook-Fisher
Baldwin Marsh 101
Dawn Ellner
Vikingsholm 101
Jonathan Cook-Fisher
Baldwin Marsh 101
Tom Purves
Eagle Falls 101
Larry & Terry Page
Western Chipmunk 105
Woods People
Yarrow 105
Steven Miller
Jeffrey Pine 105, 125, 205
The Greater Southwestern Exploration Company
Calaveras Big Trees 108
Mother of the Forest 109
David Renwald
Pacific Dogwood 109
Peter & Joyce Grace
Father of the Forest 109
THX0477
Moaning Caverns 112

Edward Stojakovic
Yosemite 116
Veit
Mule Deer 117, 125
Jeff Sullivan
Climbers El Cap 117
Thejas
Meadow 117
Daniel Berna
Black Bear 117
Ron Reiring
Mono Lake 120
Sergio Ruiz
Tufa 121
Rollie Rodriguez
Golden Osprey Nest 121
djpmapleferryman
Brine Shrimp 121
Charles Ng
Devils Postpile 124
Tobin
Sierra Gooseberry 125
Blake Carroll
Columnar Basalt 125
Renee Grayson
Lichen 129
SridharSaraf
General Grant Tree 133
CHeitz
Shattered Sequoia 133
Nick Varvel
Douglas Squirrel 137
Bob Dass
Death Valley 142
Shayan
Sand Dunes 143
Fabio Achilli
Salt Flat 143
Jeff
Beetle Tracks 143
Strange Ones
Alluvial Fans
Death Valley 143
John Fowler
Red Rock Canyon State Park 146
Homer Edward
Silver Cholla 147
Rennett Stowe
Antelope Valley Poppy 150
Kevin Gill
California Poppy 151
tdlucas5000
Grape Soda Lupine 151
Crabchick
Bumblebee 151
Kev Chapman
Syrphid Flies, Hoverfly 151
Don Graham
Palm Springs Tram 154
Eric Chan
Palm Springs Tram 155
Eric Ellingson
Steller Jay 155

Eric Gropp
Whiteheaded Woodpecker 155
S. Rae
Sugar Pine 155
Lodgepole Pine 129, 155
Steven dosRemedios
Indian Canyons Oasis 158
Brian
Oasis Water 159
Marion Hobbs
Armored Stink Beetle 159
Rob Bertholf
California Barrel Cactus 159
Renee Grayson
Desert Tortoise 163
Paul
Chuckwalla 163
Christopher Michel
Joshua Tree 166
Polar Bear 217
lhogue46
Mojave Yucca 167
Carlfbagge
Skull Rock 167
Fluff Berger
Teddy Bear Cholla 167
Greg Schechter
Desert Cottontail 167
Tristan Schmurr
Cairn 171
Shaan Hurley
Slot Canyon 171
Robert Cudmore
Ocotillo 171
cultivar143
Desert Agave 175
Dawn Endico
Desert Dandelion 175
Rob Bertholf
Full Dragon 175
Kevin Dooley
Salton Sea 178
Robin L
Fish Bone 179
Judy Gallegher
great blue heron 179
RichardBH
Cattail 179
Plant Image Library
Cottonwood Tree 185
Patrick Alexander
Rattlesnake 163, 185
Malcolm Manners
Creosote 185
Glasseyes View
Shale 189
Santa Monica Mountains National Recreation Area
Boney Mountain 188
Chumash Ap House 189
Western Fence Lizard 189
Sarah
Damselfy 189
Marty B
Solstice Canyon 192

Bernard DUPONT
Nanday Parakeet 193
NatureServe
Tree of Heaven 193
Liz West
Black Mustard 193
Jeff Turner
Vasquez Rocks 196
Kris Awesome
Pictographs 197
Alex Ford
Desert Varnish 197
Jeremy Thompson
Switzer Falls 200
Rob Hannawacker
Western Whiptail Lizard 201
David Merrett
Western Gray Squirrel 201
JordanEightySeven
Alder Tree Bark 201
Jim Morefield
Bush Chinquapin 205
Gilaman
Common Sagebrush Lizard 205
Chris Hunkeler
Oceanside 208
Don Henise
Pacific Sand Crabs 209
Mike van Dalen
Surfer Kid 209
U.S. Fish and Wildlife Service Headquarters
Brown Pelican 209
Osbornb
Torrey Pines Beach 212
Mary Witzig
Torrey Pines 213
OCParks
Black Sage 213
Melissa McMasters
CA Barrel Cactus 213
Sergei Gussev
Cliffs 213
zoofanatic
Ring Tailed Lemur 217
Jon Mountjoy
Elephant Side View Walking 217
Daniel Ramirez
Orangutan 217
Jay Iwasaki
Gray Whale 220, 221
David Slater
Pelican 221
Jeffry
Sailboat 221
Jolene Thompson
Common Dolphin 221

Made in the USA
Las Vegas, NV
22 June 2024